MARLEY'S GHOST

Another Christmas Carol

I0139744

Jeff Goode

BROADWAY PLAY PUBLISHING INC
New York
www.broadwayplaypublishing.com
info@broadwayplaypublishing.com

MARLEY'S GHOST
© Copyright 2006 Jeff Goode

Cover art: Lee Moyer
First printing: January 2006
I S B N: 978-0-88145-294-5
Book design: Marie Donovan
Word processing: Microsoft Word
Typographic controls: Ventura Publisher
Typeface: Palatino
Printed and bound in the U S A

MARLEY'S GHOST was produced in November 2003 by Circle X Theater Company (Producing Artistic Directors Tara Flynn and Tim Wright, production produced by Ken Metz and Stan Weightman Jr) at the Hollywood Forever Cemetery (CA). The cast and creative contributors were:

PHANTOM . . . . Richard Augustine
HOUSEKEEPER/MRS CRATCHIT . . . . Rebecca Avery
TUTTLE . . . . Anthony Backman
GRAVEDIGGER'S WIFE/BELLE/BELLE . . . . Emma Barton
SCROOGE/YOUNG SCROOGE . . . . Bob Clendenin
GRAVEDIGGER/BEGGAR . . . . Ahmad Enani
DIMINUTIVE GHOST . . . . Kevin Fabian
MARLEY/YOUNG MARLEY . . . . Keythe Farley
BOB CRATCHIT . . . . Matt Ford
PAWNBROKER/MARGARET . . . . Jennifer Kays
JENNY/MRS FEZZIWIG . . . . Ally LoPrete
WILKINS . . . . Ross Mackenzie
GIANT GHOST . . . . Johanna McKay
REVEREND . . . . Todd Sible
LAUNDRESS/TINY TIM . . . . David Paul Wichert

Understudies: Anthony Backman, Beatrice Casini, Tom Elliott, Joe Tyler Gold, Chris LoPrete, Ross MacKenzie, Tara Platt, Jessica Toth

Director . . . . Matthew Bretz
Production Design . . . . Gary Smoot
Lighting Design . . . . Geoff Korf
Soundscape . . . . Paul Hepker
Costume Design . . . . Cynthia Herteg
Stage Manager . . . . Christi Vadovic

MARLEY'S GHOST was also produced in November 2003 by Pantheatrics at the TripleForce Artistic Center, Columbus OH. The cast and creative contributors were:

REVEREND/PHANTOM . . . . Richard Isbell
SCROOGE . . . . Michael Wilson
GRAVEDIGGER'S WIFE/MRS FEZZIWIG . Megan Cooper
GRAVEDIGGER/PAWNBROKER . . . . .Richard Napoli
MARLEY . . . . Rene Saxton
WILKINS/BEGGAR . . . . Eric Ewing
TUTTLE . . . . David Belskie
BOB CRATCHIT . . . . Justin Moon
JENNY/BELLE/LAUNDRESS . . . . .Courtney DeCosky
HOUSEKEEPER/MRS CRATCHIT . . . . .Yvonne Isbell
GIANT GHOST . . . . Michael Parsons
DIMINUTIVE GHOST . . . . Kendra Lyn
YOUNG MARLEY . . . . .James Logan
YOUNGSCROOGE . . . . Isaac Nippert
MARGARET . . . . Christie Pitko
TINY TIM . . . . Amanda Ciani
CRATCHIT CHILDREN . . . . Brianna Biffath,
                    Devin Isbell, Katelyn Whitted

Director . . . . Dale Gregory
Production manager . . . . Arnie Thies
Stage managers . . . . Isaac Nippert,
                    Courtney DeCosky & Eric Ewing
House Manager . . . . .Joyce Thies

PRODUCTION NOTES

Scenery and characters come and go as effortlessly as phantoms throughout the play, because, unlike SCROOGE's tale, which begins in the natural world, MARLEY's adventure occurs entirely within the ghostly realm from start to finish. For MARLEY is dead...to begin with.

The PHANTOM, the GIANT GHOST and the DIMINUTIVE GHOST are character designations for the three ghosts, borrowed from Dickens' descriptions in the original novel. However, the physical appearance of these characters is not integral to the plot of MARLEY'S GHOST, and should not be taken as a requirement of this script.

If the play is performed in repertory with an ongoing production of A CHRISTMAS CAROL, it may be preferable to use the costumes already designed for those characters, regardless of whether they are diminutive or gigantic or phantasmal.

The playwright always encourages color-blind and gender-blind casting—choosing the best actor for the role, regardless of their own personal race or gender. The fact that SCROOGE is an elderly British man does not necessarily mean that the actor playing him has to be.

INTERMISSION

If you wish to add an act break, the JUDGE can simply call a short recess at any time, and then gavel the court back in session after the break. The author recommends an intermission after the BELLE and SCROOGE scene, at the end of page 46. To wit:

DIMINUTIVE GHOST: What is it that misery loves, your honor?

(The GIANT GHOST *unexpectedly bursts into tears.)*

GIANT GHOST: The Court will take a short recess to compose itself.

(The GIANT GHOST *sobs and runs out of the room.)*

END OF ACT ONE

ACT TWO *then commences with:*

GIANT GHOST: *(Gaveling)* Court is now in session. Order! Order! Now, if there is nothing further from the prosecution?

1. MARLEY'S FUNERAL

(A cemetery outside of London. Before an open grave.
REVEREND HEDGES performs the ceremony.
A GRAVEDIGGER and his WIFE wait nearby with shovels.
EBENEZER SCROOGE is the sole mourner.)

REVEREND: We are gathered here today to lay to rest
the earthly remains of our dear departed brother Jacob
Timothy Marley. May he rest in peace. What can one
say about a man like Jacob Marley...?

(Pause. He looks around helplessly, at a loss for words. No
one offers any suggestions, so...)

REVEREND: Amen.

(SCROOGE comes over to shake the REVEREND's hand.)

SCROOGE: Beautiful ceremony, Reverend. Very concise.
Economy of words. He would have liked that.

REVEREND: You must be the next of kin.

SCROOGE: I'm his business partner, yes. Ebenezer
Scrooge.

REVEREND: Oh good, because there is still a bit of
business to attend to.

SCROOGE: What's that?

REVEREND: The fee.

SCROOGE: What fee?

REVEREND: For the service.

SCROOGE: I wasn't aware that I had done you a service.

REVEREND: The memorial service. The blessing upon his soul.

SCROOGE: Oh, that. Think nothing of it, Reverend. I am happy to oblige. Yours is not a breed of superstition I particularly subscribe to. But the rituals are amusing enough, and seemingly harmless overall. And we would have buried him anyway, so it wouldn't be right to charge you for it.

REVEREND: Charge me?! I'll have you know, Mister Scrooge, that the laying to rest of the deceased is neither superstitious, nor amusing. it is one of the most sacred and fundamental sacraments in all of Christendom. That's why one hires a clergyman to perform it.

SCROOGE: Hires?

REVEREND: Yes, hires.

SCROOGE: You don't expect me to *pay* you for exploiting the occasion of my dear partner's death to practice your bizarre and antiquated customs over his helpless corpse?

REVEREND: There is nothing bizarre or antiquated about commending the spirit to the hereafter.

SCROOGE: The human spirit is a humbug.

REVEREND: A humb—?? Your language, Mister Scrooge! I am a minister. And there are ladies present.

SCROOGE: Minister, indeed! A minister of finance! If I had known that your interest in Jacob Marley's soul was purely mercenary, I would have put a stop to it immediately. This is a *funeral*, sir.

REVEREND: Yes! I know! I performed the service!

SCROOGE: A service you perform only for the wealthy dead, I take it, and those with a pocketful of change to scavenge. What happens to the poor and indigent? Cast into the Thames with a stone about their necks?

REVEREND: Of course not. Every soul is equal in the eyes of heaven, regardless of wealth or stature. But I hope you're not suggesting that His Divine Magnanimity excuses your debt to the church?

SCROOGE: I hope you're not suggesting that I pay you for a service you would have performed anyway, with or without my consent.

REVEREND: That is precisely what I am suggesting, Mister Scrooge. I came here in good faith, in your time of need, to say a few words over your friend—

SCROOGE: If words are your commerce, then you should do as any manufacturer of defective products, and take them back, for I have no use for them.

REVEREND: I do take them back! May he *never* rest in peace. And may you never find it either, so long as you walk this Earth. Nor ever after.

SCROOGE: Bah!

REVEREND: You are an affront to humanity and decency, Mister Scrooge—you, and any man like you.

SCROOGE: I'm glad you got that off your chest. Now get out of my sight before I charge you a physician's fee for the therapeutic release.

REVEREND: This miscourtesy will haunt you, Ebenezer Scrooge.

SCROOGE: Bah!

(The REVEREND *storms out. He storms back in.)*

REVEREND: Merry Christmas.

SCROOGE: Humbug!

(The REVEREND *exits again. The* GRAVEDIGGER *nudges his* WIFE. *She reluctantly approaches* SCROOGE.*)*

WIFE: Excuse me. Mister Scrooge, is it? Mayhap you will remember me? I am the wife of the gravedigger.

SCROOGE: What's that to me?

WIFE: My husband asked me to speak to you.

SCROOGE: What kind of man is he that he cannot speak for himself?

WIFE: He's a deaf mute man, sir.

SCROOGE: Ah. Yes, that's right. What is it then?

WIFE: Well, we couldn't help overhearing your quarrel with the Reverend.

(The GRAVEDIGGER nods and points.)

SCROOGE: And now you're wondering if I intend to pay your fees, as well? You needn't worry. Ebenezer Scrooge always settles his debts. (Reaching for his purse) Now, how much was it again?

WIFE: Nine shillings, sir.

SCROOGE: The price you quoted me this summer was six.

WIFE: But that was months ago. We thought you wanted him buried then.

SCROOGE: He wasn't dead then.

WIFE: Then why were you asking about it? You're not involving us in some grisly undertaking, are you? ...Because that'll cost you extra.

SCROOGE: Nothing of the sort. A good businessman is prepared for every contingency, that is all: Sudden illness. Fall from a horse. Swallowed some arsenic. Do you wait until the bodies arrive at the cemetery to start digging a hole?

WIFE: Of course, we do.

SCROOGE: Well, you see, that's poor planning. That's why you live in a little cottage here on the cemetery grounds. You would do better to dig your holes in summer when the ground is soft. Opportunity, madam.

WIFE: But it's winter now and the ground is hard. ...And it's Christmas!

SCROOGE: What the devil does that matter? I was promised one grave, dug and filled, for six shillings, and I'll not be swindled out of a penny more.

WIFE: And we won't bury him for less than nine. We'll not be swindled either, Mister Scrooge.

SCROOGE: Well, then we are at a stalemate.

WIFE: Aye, that we are. If stalemate means what I think it does.

(The GRAVEDIGGER interjects. When he speaks, he is not intelligible.)

GRAVEDIGGER: [It's a deadlock. In a game of chess. When neither player can win and neither player can lose, so the game ends in a draw.]

(They both stare at him.)

SCROOGE: I have an idea how we might settle this. *(Handing her his business card:)* This is my business address. And my residence. As you can see, it is a suite of offices in the mercantile district on the far side of London. It is my suggestion, therefore, that we leave him to rot in the open air, if you like, next to your cottage, and we shall see which of us is first overcome by the stench. *(He takes back his business card.)*

WIFE: You are a wicked, wicked man, Mister Scrooge.

SCROOGE: Then you would do well not to cross me, cross me, Mrs Gravedigger.

(SCROOGE exits. The WIFE scowls.)

GRAVEDIGGER: [What are we going to do now?]

WIFE: Well, we can't just leave him! The old miser's right, he'll stink up the whole boneyard. But there's no point in exerting ourselves on a proper burial. Throw a layer of dirt on him to soak up the stink and leave it at that. *(She turns to go.)*

GRAVEDIGGER: [And where are you going?]

WIFE: I'm going into the house.

(The GRAVEDIGGER grumbles.)

WIFE: To bake us a pie, sweeting. It's still Christmas, after all! Or had you forgotten?

(He blushes and nods as he starts to dig, and she goes off into the cottage.)

(The GRAVEDIGGER throws a shovelful of dirt into the hole. Suddenly, JACOB MARLEY sits up out of the grave, spitting dirt, and screaming like he has awakened from a very bad dream.)

MARLEY: HAAAAAAAAAAHH!!

(The GRAVEDIGGER continues shoveling, as if nothing has happened.)

MARLEY: Merciful Hades, what a nightmare. I dreamed I was being buried alive by a hideous hen-pecked deaf mute. *(Realizing:)* Wait a moment, where am I? What am I doing in a graveyard? In my bedclothes? On a Saturday? How did I get here? *(Noticing the GRAVEDIGGER)* And who are you?

(The GRAVEDIGGER, oblivious to him, continues shoveling.)

MARLEY: Answer me, Man!

(The GRAVEDIGGER stops shoveling and walks away.)

MARLEY: Where are you going? Don't walk away from me! Do you know who I am? I am Jacob Marley!

(But the GRAVEDIGGER *is already gone.)*

MARLEY: Oh no... He's a deaf mute. Just like in my dream. How is this happening? This had better not be one of Bob's pranks. *(Loudly)* Do you hear me, Bob Cratchit? *(No response)* Bob? *(Nothing)* Nephew? *(Still nothing)* I'd better not find out you've dragged me off to a graveyard in the middle of the night and left me there. Alone. Without even someone around to pinch me to see if I'm dreaming.

*(*MARLEY *hears someone approaching.)*

MARLEY: What's that? Who's out there? *(Recognizing:)* That ghostly presence... That deathly pale complexion! ...Is that you, Ebenezer?

(Enter the PHANTOM—*a hooded spirit who* SCROOGE *will later come to know as the Ghost of Christmas Yet to Come.)*

MARLEY: There you are, Scrooge. You nearly startled me, creeping about in the dark like that. Come, help your old partner out of this hole he's got himself into. I've just had the most harrowing nightmare. And you were in it. And that Reverend Hedges. Do you remember him? The one who owes us money. And there was a wretched funeral in my dream. I wonder who it was for—

*(*PHANTOM *pinches him.)*

MARLEY: Ow! You pinched me! What was that for? Wait a minute! You're not Scrooge! You're not my partner. Who are you? What do you want with me?

(The PHANTOM *beckons.)*

MARLEY: What? You want me to come with you?

(The PHANTOM *beckons more emphatically.)*

MARLEY: No, I'm not going anywhere. Not with the likes of you.

(The PHANTOM *shrugs, "Why not?")*

MARLEY: Why not? Because you're wandering around
a graveyard draped in black like some ghastly undead
spirit sent to torment the living, for one thing.

(PHANTOM *shakes its head "no".)*

MARLEY: Oh, you're not here to torment the living?

(PHANTOM *points at* MARLEY)

MARLEY: You're here to torment me? That's very funny,
"Spirit." Very amusing. Well, I'm afraid you're going
to have to torment me some other time, because I'm
clearly not feeling well this evening. I wonder if I
have a fever. That would certainly explain this vivid
delirium. But more likely it's something I ate. Or
something I didn't eat. I always suffer the most morbid
fantasies when I miss my evening meal. It's my penance
for working so late. But that's the curse of the successful
businessman. Yes, now that I think about it, I was
having the most excruciating stomach pangs as I took
to my bed. That must be it. So you see, Spirit, you are
merely a figment of my indigestion. There's nothing so
spectral about you that it can't be exorcised with a spot
of tea and a sandwich the moment I wake from this
dream.

(PHANTOM *pinches him again.)*

MARLEY: Ouch! You pinched me again! *(Sudden
realization:)* Again? You pinched me before and I
felt that, too. ...Oh no.

(PHANTOM *nods, "Oh yes.")*

MARLEY: But that would mean...?

(PHANTOM *nods again.)*

MARLEY: But that's impossible. No, it can't be. I can't be
not dreaming. *(He pinches himself on the arm.)* Ow.

(PHANTOM *pinches him, too.*)

MARLEY: Ow. *(He pinches himself again)* Ow.

(PHANTOM *pinches him, too.*)

MARLEY: Ow. Stop it! No more pinching!

(PHANTOM *signals "Truce".*)

MARLEY: So I'm not asleep. Is that it? But what am I to make of this? How can this be real? And how did I come to be spirited out of my bed and transported across town and left standing in an open grave in my bed clothes? And why? And how? And who are you? And who's grave is this? And what does any of this have to do with me?

(PHANTOM *points at the tombstone. Lightning flashes.*)

MARLEY: What? The tombstone? What about it?

(PHANTOM *points at the tombstone again. More lightning.*)

MARLEY: No, I don't want to read the inscription. Just tell me what it says.

(PHANTOM *continues to gesture more and more emphatically.*)

MARLEY: I don't want to look. What does it say? Who is buried here? Tell me, Spirit! Speak to me! Whose grave is this? *(He falls to his knees, covering his eyes and sobbing.)* ...Just tell me! Who is dead?

(Exasperated, the PHANTOM *waves its hand and suddenly they are transported to...)*

(An office in a counting-house...where two businessmen, DICK WILKINS *and* BENJAMIN TUTTLE, *are meeting.)*

WILKINS: Merry Christmas, Tuttle!

TUTTLE: Merry Christmas to you, Mister Wilkins! And a happy New Year!

WILKINS: And a prosperous one, too, by the looks of it. Now that we're here.

MARLEY: Tuttle and Wilkins? *(He ducks behind the* PHANTOM *to avoid being seen.)* Ahem. Former business associates of mine. What are they doing *here*?

WILKINS: Yes, I never thought I'd see the day.

TUTTLE: Marley swore neither of us would ever set foot in his counting-house as long as he lived.

MARLEY: Indeed, I did.

TUTTLE: And here we are.

MARLEY: The counting-house? *(Glancing around in a panic, he suddenly realizes that it is the office of his own counting-house of Marley & Scrooge.)* How did we get here? *(To* TUTTLE *and* WILKINS*)* Get out! Get out, you! This minute! Or I'll have you apprehended as trespassers!

(But neither TUTTLE *nor* WILKINS *seems to hear him.)*

TUTTLE: So you've heard the news, of course?

WILKINS: Yes, of course.

MARLEY: What news? What have you heard?? *(To the* PHANTOM*)* Why won't anyone listen to me today?

*(*PHANTOM *gestures, "Ssh! Be quiet. Listen.")*

TUTTLE: Are you going to the funeral?

WILKINS: On Christmas day? I think that man has ruined enough of my holidays without me giving him one more to spoil posthumously.

*(*MARLEY *waves his hands in front of them, but they cannot see him.)*

MARLEY: What are these? Some insensible visions that can neither see nor hear?

(PHANTOM *does not answer, pointing instead to the door where* BOB CRATCHIT *is about to come in, followed by his assistant,* JENNY.)

BOB: Oh, hello.

MARLEY: My nephew Bob! He'll put a stop to this.

WILKINS: What about you, Bob Cratchit? Going to the funeral?

BOB: No, sir, I have work.

WILKINS: On Christmas day?

BOB: Well, there's more to do now.

TUTTLE: You ought to think about taking on extra help.

BOB: Well, our Jenny here has been a real blessing.

MARLEY: Ha! The girl is incompetent. I don't know why I hired her.

TUTTLE: But what you need is another clerk.

BOB: I'm afraid there's no budget for it. Mister Scrooge says it's the economy.

TUTTLE: That Scrooge is becoming every bit as stingy as his partner.

WILKINS: I wouldn't say Marley was stingy...shrewd, yes.

TUTTLE: Frugal.

WILKINS: Yes. Tight-fisted.

TUTTLE: Penny-pinching.

WILKINS: Money grubbing.

MARLEY: Heh heh heh. I *am* all that.

TUTTLE: Miserly.

WILKINS: Malicious.

TUTTLE: Insidious.

WILKINS: Vicious.

MARLEY: That's enough!

TUTTLE: Insufferable.

WILKINS: Malignant.

TUTTLE: Diabolical.

WILKINS: Malignant.

(Thye laugh.)

MARLEY: Now you have gone too far! I don't care if I am invisible to you, I want the both of you out of my counting-house this instant! Spirit, do something! You can't let them talk about me behind my back like this, right before my eyes. *(To* TUTTLE *and* WILKINS*)* So help me, Gentlemen, when I am tangible again, I shall expunge you like a bad credit.

TUTTLE: You know, you said malignant twice.

WILKINS: Yes, but I enjoyed it so much the first time. Ha ha ha!

JENNY: *(Loudly indignant:)* Gentlemen, for shame! The way you talk! I happen to think that Mister Marley is the sweetest, kindest, most generous man I have ever had the pleasure of knowing.

MARLEY: I always liked her. Very capable.

JENNY: And it's a crime the two of you speaking ill of him.

MARLEY: Indeed!

WILKINS: He cannot hear you, Jenny. He's dead.

MARLEY: You will certainly wish I were when I get ahold of you!

JENNY: Are you sure?

TUTTLE: Dead as a doornail.

JENNY: This isn't one of Bob Cratchit's pranks?

BOB: I wouldn't joke about that, Jenny. He's really dead this time.

MARLEY: Dead?

JENNY: You're sure? This isn't another trick?

MARLEY: Bah! *One time* I counterfeit a death certificate for insurance purposes. And I have yet to hear the end of it.

JENNY: You're absolutely certain?

WILKINS & TUTTLE: Yes!!

JENNY: Well, good, because that man was the very devil.

TUTTLE: That's the spirit!

WILKINS: And his partner's no better, trust me.

JENNY: Between the three of them, I don't know who's the worse.

TUTTLE: Three?

JENNY: Marley or Scrooge or the devil himself.

WILKINS: Ha ha ha! That's a slander, Jenny.

TUTTLE: Against the devil! Ha ha ha!

JENNY: I never thought I'd live to see a more hateful couple of scoundrels than Mister Marley and Mister Scrooge. Spiteful, inhospitable, good for nothing—

WILKINS: Careful now, Jenny, Scrooge still walks among us.

JENNY: —nothing but bringing joy into the lives of all they meet.

(SCROOGE *has just come in.* TUTTLE *and* WILKINS *stop laughing.*)

SCROOGE: Mister Tuttle, Mister Wilkins... Please step into my office, we have long overdue business to conduct.

MARLEY: Business? With them? After what I've done to them?? Or rather, what they've done to me? Don't you dare, Ebenezer! This goes against our charter. I forbid it!

SCROOGE: And Jenny?

JENNY: Yes, Mister Scrooge, sir?

SCROOGE: You are dismissed.

JENNY: I'm done for the day? Thank you, Mister Scrooge!

SCROOGE: You are done forever. Pack your things and be gone by the end of business. And clear out your room at the worker's hostel. If you don't care for my hospitality, we shall see how living in the street suits you.

JENNY: But...but sir, it's Christmas.

SCROOGE: Then your Christmas wish had better be that the devil and I do not bring a civil action against you for slander.

(SCROOGE *laughs, coldly.* TUTTLE *and* WILKINS *laugh, too, uneasily, as they go off into* SCROOGE's *office.*)

MARLEY: But whose funeral do you suppose they meant?

(*The* PHANTOM *waves its arm again as the business people disappear and they are again standing in a...*)

(*Cemetery outside of London. The* GRAVEDIGGER *and his* WIFE *come out of their cottage.*)

WIFE: Come on, let's get it over with. Get him up out of there.

(*The* GRAVEDIGGER *climbs down into the open grave.*)

WIFE: Lucky I made arrangements with a doctor at the medical school. He pays good money for fresh corpses to be chopped up by the interns. "Cadavers" he calls 'em. He'll pay two crowns a head if all the parts are there. There was a dog sniffin' about earlier, I hope he didn't get at him.

GRAVEDIGGER: [It looks like he's all here.]

WIFE: Stop dallying then, and heave him up quick. I've still got stuffing to make if we're having company over.

(They haul a shrouded body out of the grave and drag it away.)

MARLEY: Where are you going? This is grave robbery! Spirit, can you do nothing to prevent this abomination? That poor, wretched man! ...Whoever he is.

(Shaking its head in disbelief, the PHANTOM waves its hand again and...)

(A pawnbroker's parlour appears. The proprietor, a furtive old crone, goes to the door and calls into the antechamber.)

PAWNBROKER: Let the laundress come next. Then the undertaker's man after that. And the charwoman may follow third.

(A LAUNDRESS with a huge bundle follows the PAWNBROKER into the parlour.)

PAWNBROKER: Come into the parlour, Mrs Neuman. I've been expecting a visit from you since I heard of his death.

LAUNDRESS: I would have been here sooner, but that old Scrooge has hardly left his bedside, watching over him like a carrion bird.

MARLEY: Is it a friend of Scrooge who has died, Spirit? That would explain his erratic business dealings. Sorrow must have addled his brain. It's not his nephew Fred, is it? He pampers that boy, you know.

(*The* PHANTOM *pinches him again.*)

MARLEY: Ow!

PAWNBROKER: So what do you have for me?

LAUNDRESS: Undo the bundle there and see.
I came straight from the dead man's house.

(PAWNBROKER *pulls some curtains out of the bundle.*)

PAWNBROKER: What do you call this? Bed-curtains?

LAUNDRESS: Aye. Bed-curtains.

PAWNBROKER: You don't mean to say you took them
down, rings and all, with him lying there?

LAUNDRESS: Yes I do, why not? If he wanted to
keep them after he was dead, the wicked old screw,
why wasn't he natural in his lifetime? If he had been,
he'd have had somebody to look after him when he
was struck with Death, instead of lying gasping out
his last there, alone by himself, with that old vulture
leering over him.

PAWNBROKER: It's the truest word that ever was spoke.
It's a judgment on him.

LAUNDRESS: I certainly shan't hold my hand, when I
can get anything in it by reaching it out, for the sake of
such a man as he was, I promise you. Don't drop that
oil upon the blankets, now.

(PAWNBROKER *has pulled some blankets out of the bundle.*)

PAWNBROKER: His blankets?

LAUNDRESS: Whose else's do you think? He isn't likely
to take cold without them, I dare say.

PAWNBROKER: I hope he didn't die of anything catching.

LAUNDRESS: Don't you be afraid of that. He was in
perfect health, that one. There's not a plague in

Christendom that wouldn't choke on a bite of his bitter hide.

(PAWNBROKER *pulls a shirt out of the bundle and holds it up to the light.*)

LAUNDRESS: Ah. you may look through that shirt till your eyes ache; but you won't find a hole in it, nor a threadbare place. It's the best he had, and a fine one too. They'd have wasted it, if it hadn't been for me.

PAWNBROKER: What do you call wasting of it?

LAUNDRESS: Putting it on him to be buried in, to be sure. Somebody was fool enough to do it, but I took it off again.

PAWNBROKER: Mrs Neuman, that's inhuman! And immodest, you are a married woman.

LAUNDRESS: Oh, you are of a filthy mind. I left him in his bed clothes. Besides, if decency were a concern for him, he might have shown some of it during his lifetime.

PAWNBROKER: Ha, ha. That's true enough. He frightened every one away from him when he was alive, to profit us when he was dead. Ha, ha, ha.

MARLEY: Now I understand, Spirit, why you have visited me tonight. Poor Scrooge has suffered some terrible loss, which has deeply affected his judgement or he never would have let valuables slip out of a house right under his nose. I shall be mindful of his fragile state and strive to employ the utmost tact when I reprimand him for his irresponsible dealings with Tuttle and Wilkins.

(The PHANTOM *shakes its fists in frustration. Lightning flashes and the scene changes to...*)

(The church on the commons. The REVEREND *ushers in a shivering* HOUSEKEEPER.)

REVEREND: Come in, my child. You're freezing.
(*Puzzled*) Though it's not that cold out.

HOUSEKEEPER: It's the house I work for. We're not
allowed coal in it.

MARLEY: That's my housekeeper, Mrs Adrian!

HOUSEKEEPER: I'm sorry to disturb you at such an
ungodly hour, Reverend, and on a holiday no less,
but I have a perilous fear for my soul if I don't make
immediate confession.

REVEREND: Not to worry, the Lord never rests, and
neither does his holy church.

HOUSEKEEPER: But he rests on Sundays, doesn't he?

REVEREND: Uh... What seems to be the matter, Mrs
Adrian?

HOUSEKEEPER: I have committed a wrong so grievous
that the thought of it haunts my every waking moment
and disturbs me in my sleep with guilt of what I have
done.

REVEREND: What is it, Mrs Adrian? Tell me.

HOUSEKEEPER: This past Tuesday...I wished my
employer ill. ...And then he became ill. ...And died.

MARLEY: What rubbish! *I'm* her only employer!

REVEREND: You didn't!

HOUSEKEEPER: I did, have mercy on my soul, I did.

REVEREND: Oh, Mrs Adrian...

HOUSEKEEPER: I know I shouldn't have. I know it.
I should have held my temper. But I am only a
housekeeper, Reverend, and not a wealthy one at that,
though I work like a very beaver, I do, trying to keep
his house clean. So when he upbraided me for using too

much soap on the floorboards, and took the cost of the extra cleaning out of my salary. Well, I lost all patience.

REVEREND: What did you do?

HOUSEKEEPER: I looked him straight in the eye and said... "Yes, sir. Right away, sir. May the Lord bless and keep you, sir. ...And the sooner the better."

MARLEY: I remember that. It happened two days ago.

HOUSEKEEPER: And it was not two days later that tragedy befell him. His heart stopped. And I knew it was my doing for speaking ill of him in God's earshot.

REVEREND: That is a grave transgression, Moira.

HOUSEKEEPER: *(Sobbing)* I know it.

REVEREND: But it is good that your conscience troubles you. If it did not, I should be the more concerned.

HOUSEKEEPER: I should not have let him get to me. But Mister Marley can be such a trial sometimes.

REVEREND: Marley? Jacob Marley?!

HOUSEKEEPER: Aye, you know him, Reverend?

REVEREND: I have just now come from being robbed at his funeral by his partner!

HOUSEKEEPER: Oh, I'm sorry, Reverend.

REVEREND: The two of them hold the mortgage on this church. And last week, before he died, your Mister Marley foreclosed on it. He repossessed the church. God is being evicted from his house.

MARLEY: Heh heh. God ought to have kept up his payments.

REVEREND: If that man is dead now, I promise you his passing is no tragedy. It's an act of divine retribution, my word on it.

HOUSEKEEPER: Oh my.

REVEREND: Good riddance!

HOUSEKEEPER: Reverend!

REVEREND: If he's roasting in the fiery pits of a place
I dare not mention in the presence of God and mixed
company, it's a gentler fate than he deserves.

HOUSEKEEPER: Yes, Reverend.

REVEREND: May his unholy spirit linger forever in
perpetual damnation.

HOUSEKEEPER: Yes Reverend.

REVEREND: His decrepit soul writhing in unspeakable
torments.

HOUSEKEEPER: I understand, Reverend.

REVEREND: From now till the death of eternity.

HOUSEKEEPER: Thank you, Reverend, I feel much
relieved. He was a bastard, that Mister Marley.

REVEREND: Damn him!

HOUSEKEEPER: ...Yes.

REVEREND: Damn his infernal spirit!

HOUSEKEEPER: I'd better go now.

(As the church fades from view, the PHANTOM *turns
expectantly to* MARLEY, *who has fallen disturbingly silent.)*

MARLEY: So now I am to believe myself deceased,
is that it?

*(*PHANTOM *places a comforting hand on his shoulder,
but* MARLEY *shrugs it off.)*

MARLEY: Very funny, Spirit. Now I see your game.
Someone who thinks but little of my intelligence has
gone to a great deal of trouble to arrange this cruel and
elaborate hoax at my expense. Well, I am not a man

without humour. As you shall soon see when I catch the dickens who put you up to this, and if he is in my employ, I shall terminate him. And if he is in business, I shall bankrupt him. And if he is indebted to me, God help him, for I shall call in his debt forthwith and take possession of his home and cast him out of his bed and into the gutter and send him laughing all the way to the poor house.

(PHANTOM *tries to pinch him again, but this time* MARLEY *slaps it away.)*

MARLEY: No more of your pinching! And poking and prodding. I am not dead. Nor am I like to soon be. But you, if you touch me again, so help me... I shall have you brought up on charges of assault. In fact, I think I shall do it anyway. Constable!! I hope you have enjoyed your ghostly charade. For if you were to speak now, even to beg for mercy, nothing you could say would convince me to spare you and your accomplices from the full weight and consequence of my righteous litigation!

(The PHANTOM *points again and...)*

(The counting-house reappears. SCROOGE *enters, brandishing a freshly-painted "Marley & Scrooge" sign.)*

SCROOGE: Cratchit! Bob Cratchit!

(BOB hurries into the room.)

BOB: Yes, Mister Scrooge?

SCROOGE: I thought I told you to repaint this sign.

BOB: I did, sir. That's a fresh coat. Have a care, it's still wet.

SCROOGE: No, no, no, it's all wrong. The sign should say "Scrooge & Marley". That's what I asked for.

BOB: But, sir, it's been "Marley & Scrooge" for the past thirty-three years.

SCROOGE: Yes, and it's going to be "Scrooge & Marley" for the next thirty-three and then, if he likes, we can switch it back. Now get to it. And take the cost of the wasted paint out of your pay.

BOB: Yes, sir. "Scrooge & Marley", sir. "Scrooge & Marley".

(As BOB and SCROOGE disappear...)

(...The PHANTOM turns to MARLEY, crossing its arms in smug satisfaction.)

MARLEY: NOOOOOOOOOOOOO!!!! Spirit, what fresh horrors are these? Scrooge changing the name of the firm? That I created? He wouldn't dare to do such a thing while I'm alive. Not even in jest! Not even in a dream! (He falls to his knees.) Then it's true. I'm dead. That's what these visions are trying to tell me. Or soon shall be if I don't mend my ways. (He rises to his feet again.) Then I am resolved. First thing in the morning, I shall look to my diet. No more lavish dinners. Only dry breads and grains. And exercise! From now on I'll make two trips to the bank every day instead of one. It's probably not safe to carry that much money on me, anyway. And effective immediately, Bob Cratchit shall work double shifts on Sundays and Holidays so that I may have some time off. I mustn't overwork myself. It strains the vital organs. I don't want to end up in an early grave like the man you've shown me tonight.

(The PHANTOM turns away from him, shaking its head in consternation.)

MARLEY: But before you go, Spirit, answer me one question to ease my mind. These visions that you have shown me, are they the shadows of things that may come to pass? Or are they shadows of things that will come to pass.

(The PHANTOM *finally loses its patience, attacking and pinching him repeatedly, forcing him backward, toward the open grave.)*

MARLEY: Ow! Ow!! Ow!!!

*(*MARLEY *tumbles into the grave. The* PHANTOM *points at the tombstone again. Lightning flashes and the glowing inscription clearly reads "*JACOB MARLEY R I P"*)*

MARLEY: All right! All right! Spirit, have mercy. I can deny it no longer. I don't need to read it, Spirit. I know what it says. That is my name on the headstone. For these are things that *have* come to pass. And Jacob Marley is dead.

(The PHANTOM *throws up its hands in victory and relief, and this time, the entire graveyard swirls into the air around them and vanishes in a gust of wind and light.)*

2. THE TRIAL OF JACOB MARLEY

(Celestial Court of Imposition. MARLEY *and the* PHANTOM *finds themselves in an empty arena.)*

MARLEY: Where have you taken me now, Spirit? What is this place? Is it this future?

*(*PHANTOM *gestures "Yes and no." A gigantic ghost— who* SCROOGE *will come to know as the* GIANT GHOST— *hurries toward them, dressed as a clerk of court.)*

GIANT GHOST: *(To* PHANTOM*)* There you are! Late as usual.

*(*PHANTOM *gestures helplessly and points at* MARLEY.*)*

GIANT GHOST: Yes, yes, it's always somebody else's fault with you. *(To* MARLEY*)* And you are?

MARLEY: Jacob Marley.

GIANT GHOST: Ah! So, you're the decedent. Just in time, too, they're about to get started. Well, hurry along in, the bailiff is calling the tribunal to order even as we speak.

(MARLEY *isn't sure where "in" is supposed to be, and the* PHANTOM *just seems to meander in a circle as the* GIANT GHOST *exits and reenters wearing a bailiff's uniform.)*

GIANT GHOST: Hear ye! Hear ye! This tribunal of the 359th Celestial Court of Imposition is NOW in session! No, wait... *Now* in session! No, not yet... *(Pause)* ...NOW! Hold on... *(Takes out a pocket watch; consults it)* ...NOW!

(The GIANT GHOST *sits down and says nothing further.* MARLEY *notices a* DIMINUTIVE GHOST *sitting on a bench nearby, who seems to have been waiting for a very long time.)*

MARLEY: Have you been here long?

DIMINUTIVE GHOST: Since the dawn of time.

*(*MARLEY *takes a seat on the bench. The* GIANT GHOST *immediately stands again.)*

GIANT GHOST: All rise for the right honorable judge magistrate and tribune of the 359th Celestial Court of Imposition.

(They all rise. No one enters. The GIANT GHOST *looks around.)*

GIANT GHOST: Your honor? Is the judge magistrate present in the court room at this time? Can anyone tell me if the judge is present? *(Slaps a magistrate's wig on its head)* Yes, I am! Good evening, everyone, good morning! Please be seated. First order of business... *(Peruses the docket)* Merry Christmas! Yes, it's Christmas Day in the netherworld. Or night. Or neither. But whatever the time, now is the time for us to remember that it doesn't matter if you are bound for purgatory, or some other binding far worse than purgatory, so long as you keep Christmas in your heart, that will be one part of your anatomy that is roasting chestnuts over an open fire, and not the other way around.

MARLEY: *(Aside to the* PHANTOM*)* Christmas is a humbug.

(The GIANT GHOST *hears him and glares. The* PHANTOM *pinches* MARLEY.*)*

MARLEY: Ow!

GIANT GHOST: Second item on the docket... *(Peruses the docket)* The People versus Jacob Marley. Will the defendant please rise?

*(*PHANTOM *nudges* MARLEY.*)*

MARLEY: Me? I'm on trial? Upon what charge?

GIANT GHOST: Jacob Marley! You stand accused of crimes and misdemeanors, sins and transgressions too numerous and tedious to mention.

MARLEY: Not guilty, your honor!

GIANT GHOST: Silence! Do not interrupt, or I will be forced to hold you in more contempt than I already do.

MARLEY: But when do I respond to the charges?

GIANT GHOST: Respond? There is no response. You are here to be punished.

MARLEY: How can I be punished when I haven't been convicted?

GIANT GHOST: Your lack of convictions is precisely the problem, Jacob Marley. You are a hideous, disagreeable, curmudgeon. The facts of the indictment are beyond dispute.

MARLEY: Nonsense. *I* dispute them.

GIANT GHOST: You see? Disagreeable!

MARLEY: I am a law-abiding citizen, and an upstanding member of society—until proven otherwise. And a leader of the community, I might add.

GIANT GHOST: What community have you ever been a party to?

MARLEY: Well, the business community, of course. And the chamber of commerce. I was president of that august body once, and would be to this day, were it not for the machinations of that meddling Tuttle.

GIANT GHOST: The *business* community? Mankind was your business! The whole world was your community. Your commerce should have been with the entire human race.

MARLEY: I don't see how that would have profited me.

GIANT GHOST: Profit? Is that all you think about?

MARLEY: Yes, and I'm not ashamed to admit it. I am a tradesman by trade, skilled in the art of finance and acquisition, and proud of it. It's what I live for.

GIANT GHOST: And in the end it's what you died for.

MARLEY: What does that mean?

GIANT GHOST: Well, I've heard enough. The substance of the allegation being uncontested, and the accused demonstrating no signs of remorse—

MARLEY: Remorse for what?

GIANT GHOST: I see, therefore, no recourse but to conclude this imposition and sentence you to... ETERNITY!

MARLEY: Eternity? That seems excessive.

GIANT GHOST: In CHAINS!

MARLEY: Chains?

GIANT GHOST: CHAAAAIINS....

(An enormous curtain of ghostly chains rises out of the floor encircling MARLEY *and closing in around him.)*

GIANT GHOST: Jacob Marley, you shall walk the Earth henceforth and forever more, fettered in these chains which you forged during your lifetime. They are the chains of iniquity and avarice. Every link, every padlock, every cashbox and key, is a wrong you have committed against your fellow man. You will wear these chains about you as you wander the earth for all eternity, seeking solace where you may find it... and finding none. Next case! You are dismissed. Merry Christmas!

MARLEY: Dismissed? What about a trial? A verdict? Am I not entitled to a hearing, at least?

GIANT GHOST: You are not here to be heard. You are here to be sentenced. This is not a court of law. Those earthly games of plea and bargain are behind you now. They ended when you entered the grave.

MARLEY: But I'm not guilty!

GIANT GHOST: All men are guilty. It is only a matter of degree and consequence. In your case... *(Indicating the chains)* ...anyone can plainly see the degree of consequence your actions have warranted.

MARLEY: But surely, I have rights. Even here. I demand a trial before a jury of my peers.

GIANT GHOST: A jury? Ha ha ha! Certainly that could be arranged. But what jury would have you? Your crimes are very well known, Jacob Marley. Where do you expect to find an impartial juror to render an unbiased judgement upon your life? *(Summons images of the living to appear on the witness stand)* Shall we look among your victims?

(A WIDOW *appears on the witness stand.)*

WIDOW: After my husband succumbed to the consumption. It was so very thoughtful of Mister Marley to stop by, in person, to deliver the eviction notice. I'll never forget him for that.

MARLEY: No, not her.

(The WIDOW *vanishes. Three* FRIENDS *of* MARLEY *appear on the witness stand.)*

GIANT GHOST: Your friends and associates?

FIRST: I'm not really a friend, so much as an associate. An acquaintance, really. More of a passerby. A stranger. Yes, a total stranger.

SECOND: Never met him.

THIRD: Don't know him.

(The FRIENDS *vanish. A* BUSINESSMAN *appears on the witness stand.)*

GIANT GHOST: Your business relations?

BUSINESSMAN: I have known Jacob Marley for many, many years, and it would be an *honour* to serve as his executioner.

GIANT GHOST: Juror.

BUSINESSMAN: *(Shrugs)* Or on his jury. *(He also vanishes.)*

GIANT GHOST: Where in this world, or the next, will we find a single soul who has not suffered at your hands in one way or another?

MARLEY: Surely, that's an exaggeration. Naturally, I have competitors who resent that some transaction did not work out to their advantage, that is the nature of commerce. But I have never harmed anyone. Never committed a crime to speak of. Never been arrested, at any rate. I keep very much to myself, very much of the time.

GIANT GHOST: *That* is your crime! Every life on the earthly sphere impacts upon those around it, whether they wish it or not. You cannot lock yourself away in a counting-house and expect to do no one harm. There are crimes of omission, too, Jacob Marley. And those, you have committed in abundance. Your only hope of doing good in the world is to go out *into* the world and do good. And that you have scrupulously failed to do throughout the entirety of your life. You were never kind or outgoing. Never generous. You neglected, at every opportunity, to be merciful, or forbearing, or even moderately courteous. You walked through crowds of fellow-beings with your eyes turned down. And hoarded up all the good you might have done in life and coined it for shillings and pound notes. Stacks of paper to be sealed away in a vault. Never to be spent on anyone's well-being. Not even your own.

MARLEY: Yes, but Spirit, there must be someone who has benefited by association with me. I cannot be all so bad as that.

GIANT GHOST: One would think so. What man can navigate the vast sea of humanity without causing so much as a ripple of goodwill? But even those closest to you, cannot attest to it. Your employees... and relations...and those who were a little of both...

(BOB *appears on the witness stand.*)

MARLEY: Bob Cratchit, if you ever had a kind word for your old uncle, say it now.

BOB: My Uncle Jacob was a kind...a kind of man...who... words cannot describe.

MARLEY: Ingrate! After I took him in, and gave him a job, a trade!

GIANT GHOST: A tribulation is a better word for it. And since you failed to provide for him after your passing, his fortunes have fallen upon the tender mercies of...

(MARLEY *realizes where this is headed.*)

MARLEY: ...Ebenezer!

(SCROOGE *appears on the witness stand.* MARLEY *panics.*)

GIANT GHOST: And speaking of your life-long business partner...

MARLEY: Oh no! Don't say a word, Scrooge. You have a right to your silence.

SCROOGE: I admired and respected Jacob Marley more than any man I shall ever know. He was always an excellent man of business. A man who could truly sew a silk purse out of a sow's ear; and given a rainy day, could snatch the rainbow out of the sky and wring a pot of gold from either end. He showed me that Opportunities must be *seized*, and Profits *taken*. I would say that everything I am today, I owe to him, after a fashion. And for that, I suppose I will always be in his debt. ...So to speak.

MARLEY: Aha! You see! Some people respect me.

GIANT GHOST: Yes, out of all of humanity, Ebenezer Scrooge speaks uncompromisingly well of you. The one man whose crimes exceed yours.

(*Another set of chains—destined for* SCROOGE—*rises out of the floor, looming larger even than* MARLEY'*s)*

GIANT GHOST: The one man whose chains, when he finally reaches his day of judgement, will be far longer and heavier than yours. This is the man who vouches for your character. The man whom you have wronged more than any other. He was your partner. He called you friend. And, in the end, he murdered you.

MARLEY: What? Did you say murdered? Impossible. Scrooge wouldn't dream of such a thing.

GIANT GHOST: Ah, but what men may dream and men may do in their sleepless hours are two different things entirely.

(*The* GIANT GHOST *gestures and a vision appears...*)

(*The counting-house.* SCROOGE *enters from his office, catching* BOB *as he is about to leave for the day.*)

SCROOGE: Cratchit! Before you go—

BOB: Please, Mister Scrooge, you said I could have half a day off.

SCROOGE: (*Uncharacteristically genial*) Where's your holiday spirit, Cratchit? I have a gift for you.

BOB: Oh...

(SCROOGE *hands* BOB *a vial of poison.*)

SCROOGE: I recall you grumbling about a nest of rats infesting that house of yours. There's a vial of arsenic I won't be needing anymore. I thought you might like it.

BOB: Uh... Thank you...

SCROOGE: I would have wrapped it for you, but we wouldn't want young Tim getting into it, and thinking it a package of sweets.

BOB: No, of course not, sir.

SCROOGE: Now get home with you.

BOB: Thank you, sir.

SCROOGE: Quickly.

BOB: Yes, sir. Merry Christmas, sir!

SCROOGE: (*Can't help himself*) Bah! Humbug!

(BOB *and* SCROOGE *are gone.* MARLEY *is shaken by what he has seen.*)

MARLEY: How could he? He was my friend.

GIANT GHOST: Yes. He was your friend and co-conspirator. Your trusted cohort. Your accomplice and partner-in-crime. But enough about Scrooge. Let's talk about YOU.

(MARLEY *cringes fearfully as the* GIANT GHOST *leers down at him.*)

GIANT GHOST: *You* want a trial.

MARLEY: Perhaps a *bench* trial.

GIANT GHOST: Well, seeing as it is Christmas, and I am in a giving spirit. I see no reason why a damnéd soul should not have that which will only increase his suffering.

MARLEY: Eh?

(*With a grand sweep of its arms, the* GIANT GHOST *causes the entire courtroom to transform. The* PHANTOM, *the* GIANT GHOST *and the* DIMINUTIVE GHOST *all meander in a circle again, as the stage becomes a...*)

(*Grand Court of Inquisition ...The* GIANT GHOST *pounds with its gavel.*)

GIANT GHOST: Order! Order!! ORDER!! (*Realizes that the court has already come to order*) Ahem. This Court of Inquisition is now in session. Who speaks for the defense?

(PHANTOM *raises its hand.*)

MARLEY: But—

GIANT GHOST: Do you wish to make an opening statement?

(*The* PHANTOM *nods and rises to address the Court. Pause. It starts to speak, but stops itself. It starts to speak again, and stops. Finally, it throws up its hands and goes to sit back down.* MARLEY *glares at the* PHANTOM.)

MARLEY: You have a brilliant future in this.

(PHANTOM *nods bashfully.*)

GIANT GHOST: Very well. Then let us proceed to the prosecution.

DIMINUTIVE GHOST: Finally!

GIANT GHOST: Prosecutor, the floor is yours.

DIMINUTIVE GHOST: Thank you, your honor.

(The DIMINUTIVE GHOST *strides to the front of the room. This, by the way, is the spirit who* SCROOGE *will come to know as the Ghost of Christmas Past.)*

DIMINUTIVE GHOST: On the evening of the 25th of December, eighteen hundred and ten—

(MARLEY *leaps to his feet in a panic.)*

MARLEY: Objection!! Objection!!!

GIANT GHOST: Yes?

(MARLEY *is frozen, panic-stricken. The* PHANTOM *nudges him, but he is still speechless.)*

GIANT GHOST: Mister Marley, do you have an objection?

MARLEY: W-w-w-well...1810, why that's... So very long ago.

GIANT GHOST: Time is relative here, Jacob Marley.

MARLEY: Yes, but surely I can't be expected to remember what happened on a particular night, in a particular place, *who knows* how long ago.

DIMINUTIVE GHOST: Thirty-three years. And I'd be happy to refresh your memory.

MARLEY: Yes, but, thank you, but... is that what we're going to do here? Dredge up old memories of the long-forgotten past?

GIANT GHOST: Your whole life is the past now, Mister Marley. And, yes, some of it is likely going to be dredged.

MARLEY: But we're not going to go over every little detail of every day of every year of my entire life, are we?

GIANT GHOST: *(To the Prosecutor)* He has a point. We are already dreadfully behind schedule. And I know you have other cases.

DIMINUTIVE GHOST: That won't be a problem, your honor. I will only ask for *one* day.

GIANT GHOST: What day is that?

DIMINUTIVE GHOST: *Christmas* Day! The actions and inactions this defendant has perpetrated on that holiest of days alone, would be enough to convict a whole priesthood of men. It should more than suffice to demonstrate that this individual has deserved the just punishment that has already been set aside for him.

GIANT GHOST: That sounds fair. Christmas Day it is!

MARLEY: N-no, wait, but—

(A cloakroom in FEZZIWIG's *counting-house. The sound of music and laughter and dancing is coming from the next room.)*

DIMINUTIVE GHOST: The evening of December 25th, 1810. I'd like to have it marked and entered into evidence as People's Exhibit A.

GIANT GHOST: So noted.

DIMINUTIVE GHOST: The place, you may recognize, Mister Marley. It is a cloakroom in the counting-house where you were apprenticed. It belonged at the time to Mister Fenwick Fezziwig. Now here was a man who knew how to celebrate Christmas.

MARLEY: *(Grumbles)* Yes, yes, he was very merry.

DIMINUTIVE GHOST: But on the night in question, while Fezziwig and his other apprentices were busy in the next room, being just that. You, Jacob Marley, had ducked into this cloakroom to conduct affairs of a different sort with *Mrs* Fezziwig.

(YOUNG JACOB MARLEY sneaks into the room. He takes out a small jewelry box and fidgets nervously. Soon MRS FEZZIWIG pirouettes into the room, decked in her holiday best.)

MRS FEZZIWIG: Jacob!

(Seeing him, she throws herself into his arms and kisses him.)

YOUNG MARLEY: Mrs Fezziwig, you came!

MRS FEZZIWIG: You asked me to come.

YOUNG MARLEY: Yes, but I—

(She kisses him again.)

YOUNG MARLEY: ...Thank you.

MRS FEZZIWIG: You're welcome. But if you want to thank me properly, you ought to kiss me under the mistletoe.

YOUNG MARLEY: *(Looking up)* I don't see any mistletoe.

(She gives him a suggestive wink.)

MRS FEZZIWIG: That's because I'm wearing it.

(She starts to kiss him again, but he interrupts her.)

YOUNG MARLEY: There is something I have to ask you.

MRS FEZZIWIG: What is it, Jacob? You look so serious.

YOUNG MARLEY: I've been meaning to do this for a very long time.

(YOUNG MARLEY goes down on one knee and takes her by the hand.)

MRS FEZZIWIG: Jacob, you're kneeling. What's wrong?

YOUNG MARLEY: Mrs. Fezziwig... I am planning to go
out on my own very soon. To start my own business.

MRS FEZZIWIG: You're leaving the company?
Mister Fezziwig will be very disappointed. *(Realizing)*
...Or is it *me* that you are leaving?

YOUNG MARLEY: No, Mrs Fezziwig, not at all.
...Not if you come with me.

MRS FEZZIWIG: What?

YOUNG MARLEY: Tonight. While everyone is in at the
Christmas party indulging in their holiday revels.

MRS FEZZIWIG: Jacob, I am a married woman.

YOUNG MARLEY: But you don't love him. You love me.

MRS FEZZIWIG: Oh, Jacob... *(She strokes his cheek)* I'm
sorry if you have misinterpreted my affections. Despite
what you may think, I do love Mister Fezziwig. It's true
that he leaves something to be desired in the husbandry
department. But so long as those desires can be satisfied
in the *accounting* department, I see no reason to upset
the order of things. You are a sweet boy, Jacob. And
I shall miss you if you go. But do not ask me to break
my marriage contract, for my answer to that must be
"no".And I will enjoy the holidays so much better with
you here.

YOUNG MARLEY: I see. *(He stands, straightens his
coattails.)* I was afraid you might say that. I had
hoped against it. ...But I did fear it. *(He takes out a
legal document.)* I did not want to do this, Mrs Fezziwig.
Believe me when I say that it was the furthest thing
from my mind when I asked you here tonight.

MRS FEZZIWIG: And yet you drew up what appears to
be a lengthy legal document.

YOUNG MARLEY: Since contracts are what you respect, that is what we shall have between us.

MRS FEZZIWIG: What is the meaning of this, Jacob?

YOUNG MARLEY: Mrs Fezziwig, your husband is not a competent man of business. But you knew that when you married him. Your father knew it, too, which is why he left the family business in *your* name. Despite your father's precautions, however, you have allowed your husband to run the company into the ground, and as a result, the Fezziwig concern will be bankrupt within the year. I know this, because I am the one keeping the books. I know it, also, because I have been embezzling funds from your husband's accounts for the past six months in order to hasten the demise of Fezziwig and Company.

MRS FEZZIWIG: What! If this is true, I will have you jailed for it!

YOUNG MARLEY: As your accountant, I would advise against that. Imprisoning me will not recover the funds I have secreted away. The business will still collapse. And when it does, you shall join me in prison. Debtor's prison.

MRS FEZZIWIG: No!

YOUNG MARLEY: I have a proposal, however, which will spare you that inglorious fate and serve my own ends as well. You see, I, too, have a small problem in that I cannot make use of the monies I have stolen from you without a legitimate business front to mask my sudden surplus income from the banking authorities. *(He shows her the contract and hands her a fountain pen.)* By signing control of your company over to me, you solve both of our problems. Without me siphoning off assets, the business will revive and, in fact, prosper under my capable management. And you and Mister Fezziwig will survive on the modest pension you receive as minority shareholders in Marley and Company.

MRS FEZZIWIG: I have a counterproposal. I shall inform my husband of your duplicity. And he will have you taken out into the courtyard and thrashed soundly and repeatedly until you divulge the whereabouts of the missing funds of your own volition.

YOUNG MARLEY: Then I hope, for your sake, that while I am having the truth beaten out of me, I do not also let slip the name of my lover, as I cry out to her for mercy, in the name of the passion we once shared.

MRS FEZZIWIG: You wouldn't dare!

YOUNG MARLEY: Don't be such a pessimist. I suspect that I would dare.

MRS FEZZIWIG: I shall deny it.

YOUNG MARLEY: Will you deny also the strawberry-shaped birthmark beneath your left bosom? Or the suggestive arrangement of mistletoe you are currently wearing in a garland about your waist? Or the indecent bite mark which I left only yesterday astride your starboard buttock?

MRS FEZZIWIG: You monster!

YOUNG MARLEY: So you have created me. But sign the paper, Mrs Fezziwig. And all of your monsters will remain safely cloaked in their shadows.

(*Just then,* YOUNG EBENEZER SCROOGE *bursts in on them.*)

YOUNG SCROOGE: Marley, there you are!

YOUNG MARLEY: Scrooge!

YOUNG SCROOGE: And Mrs Fezziwig. What are you doing in here?

YOUNG MARLEY: Never mind that. Go back to the party.

YOUNG SCROOGE: But they're opening the presents.

YOUNG MARLEY: We'll be there in a minute.

YOUNG SCROOGE: Mister Fezziwig is calling for both of you. He sent me to find you. And Dick Wilkins is searching the whole the house.

YOUNG MARLEY: I said, get out!

(But YOUNG SCROOGE, *sensing something amiss, steps further into the room, closing the door behind him.)*

YOUNG SCROOGE: What in the name of Christmas is going on in here?

(Seeing the document, YOUNG SCROOGE *seizes it, but* YOUNG MARLEY *stops him.)*

YOUNG MARLEY: Ebenezer... You have come upon us at an inopportune moment. But there's no reason this should not be an opportunity for you.

YOUNG SCROOGE: What do you mean?

YOUNG MARLEY: How does the name "Marley & Scrooge" sound to you?

YOUNG SCROOGE: It sounds like your name and mine put together.

YOUNG MARLEY: Yes it does. And so it shall be.
If you choose to join me. I am about to go into business for myself, Ebenezer. You could be my partner.

YOUNG SCROOGE: At what price? You know I have no savings to invest.

YOUNG MARLEY: The cost to you will be ten minutes easy labour.

YOUNG SCROOGE: Ten minutes?

YOUNG MARLEY: All I ask of you in return for a full partnership in the firm is that you leave this room

immediately. And see to it that no one else comes
through that door under any circumstances.

YOUNG SCROOGE: Not even Dick Wilkins?

YOUNG MARLEY: Especially that meddling Dick
Wilkins! ...Give me ten minutes of this service and
you will advance your career more than you could
in ten years as an apprentice, for at the end of it, you
and I will be partners in a joint venture that will more
than justify your not reading this paper, not asking
any questions, and not hesitating another moment.

(YOUNG SCROOGE *eyes them both suspiciously, then he
slowly backs out of the room.* YOUNG MARLEY *hands*
MRS FEZZIWIG *the paper and the pen again.*)

YOUNG MARLEY: Sign the paper, Mrs Fezziwig.
Then we cab both get down to the business of
enjoying the holidays.

(*She starts to sob as she signs. The vision fades into shadows.*)

DIMINUTIVE GHOST: Poor Mister Fezziwig. He had no
idea?

MARLEY: Oh, you needn't pity him, or his wife either
for that matter. She reconciled with him, shortly
thereafter, and the experience brought them closer
together. In the end, they both died merry and happy.
And *penniless.*

DIMINUTIVE GHOST: Well, poor Scrooge then. Drawn
into this sordid business with you.

MARLEY: You think I tricked him into it? He and Dick
Wilkins had talked of doing this for years huddled in
their little accountant's cells.

DIMINUTIVE GHOST: Blackmailing Mrs Fezziwig?

MARLEY: No! Starting a business. Going off on their
own. We all would have done it eventually, one way or

another, I merely spared us decades of toiling away our youths making other men rich, and ourselves miserable.

DIMINUTIVE GHOST: Instead you toiled away your youths making yourselves rich. *And* miserable.

MARLEY: Do not shed a tear for Ebenezer Scrooge for all I did was grant him his fondest wish. There's one man who cannot say I never gave him anything for Christmas.

GIANT GHOST: Let us move on to another Christmas.

DIMINUTIVE GHOST: Yes, your honor. People's Exhibit B!

(Marley & Scrooge's counting-house. A few years later. YOUNG SCROOGE *is trying to work when* YOUNG MARLEY *enters in a huff.)*

YOUNG SCROOGE: Merry Christmas, Jacob.

YOUNG MARLEY: Bah! Our profits are down another quarter.

YOUNG SCROOGE: Well, it's the economy.

YOUNG MARLEY: The economy is a humbug. One of us is not pulling his full weight.

YOUNG SCROOGE: And which one of us would that be, Jacob?

YOUNG MARLEY: I think that goes without saying.

YOUNG SCROOGE: I am here eighteen hours a day, slaving my fingers to the bone for this company. I should think that what's hurting our business more than my slothfulness is your compulsion for driving our customers away with your antisocial fits of distemper.

*(*YOUNG MARLEY, *stung, becomes dangerously quiet and sullen.* YOUNG SCROOGE *tries to ignore him.)*

YOUNG MARLEY: You have changed.

YOUNG SCROOGE: *(Trying to work)* Have I? How?

YOUNG MARLEY: When we began this enterprise, you and I, we swore on a contract that nothing would come between us and our goals for this firm. But now... *(Shrugs)* You seem distracted.

YOUNG SCROOGE: Perhaps it is the excessive talking while I'm working.

YOUNG MARLEY: I think it's *her*.

YOUNG SCROOGE: Belle is not the problem.

YOUNG MARLEY: I think she is. Or she will be. Trust me, old friend, she is a woman.

YOUNG SCROOGE: So I've noticed.

YOUNG MARLEY: One day, the feeling will come over her that you haven't loved her well enough, and she will ask you to choose between this place and her. And you will. And you will go. And then everything we have built up in so short a time will be torn down in even less.

YOUNG SCROOGE: Nonsense. I am committed to this venture. Nothing you or Belle or anyone can say is going to change that.

YOUNG MARLEY: It is kind of you to say, but it is not true. And so, Merry Christmas.

(YOUNG MARLEY *hands* YOUNG SCROOGE *a contract with a ribbon tied around it.*)

YOUNG SCROOGE: What's this?

YOUNG MARLEY: You may call it a holiday bonus. It is our contract. Tear it up if you like. Put an end to "Marley & Scrooge", if that's what you want.

YOUNG SCROOGE: Jacob...

(BELLE *walks in.*)

YOUNG MARLEY: Hello, Belle!

BELLE: Jacob, Merry Christmas.

YOUNG MARLEY: What brings you to the counting-house? Again? If this keeps up, I shall have to put you to work cleaning the place.

YOUNG SCROOGE: Jacob!

BELLE: It's all right, I'll go.

YOUNG MARLEY: No, *I'll* go. I couldn't bear to stay and see so much *work* being done around here.

(YOUNG MARLEY exits. YOUNG SCROOGE turns on BELLE.)

YOUNG SCROOGE: Now look what you've done!

BELLE: Me?

YOUNG SCROOGE: Yes, you! You know Jacob doesn't like you interfering in our business.

BELLE: Interfering?

YOUNG SCROOGE: Well, meddling.

BELLE: Meddling?!

YOUNG SCROOGE: You know what I mean.

BELLE: No, I don't Ebenezer. Perhaps you could insult me some more? I wouldn't want you to sugar-coat it.

YOUNG SCROOGE: I'm sorry. I don't mean to upset you. But you *do* know what I mean. My work is important to me, and Jacob as much as accused me just now of letting your attentions become a distraction, and yet you persist in always being...

BELLE: What? Attentive?

YOUNG SCROOGE: In being... *(Trying to make it a compliment)* ...distracting. *(He tries to take her in his arms.)*

BELLE: Ebenezer, do you love me still?

YOUNG SCROOGE: Bah! Why do you vex me with trivial questions when it delays my work?

BELLE: Why do you delay in answering if the question is so trivial?

YOUNG SCROOGE: Yes, of course, I do. I worship you. I cherish your every annoyance. You are the idol upon whose altar I drop my heart's blood. Now, can I finish, or would you prefer that I spend another Christmas here toiling over books that should have been done on Christmas Eve?

BELLE: What I prefer matters little. To you, very little. Another idol has replaced me in your esteem. A golden one. And if it can cheer and comfort you in time to come, as I would have tried to do, then I have no cause to grieve.

YOUNG SCROOGE: Bah! This is the great hypocrisy of the world. There is nothing on which it is so hard as poverty, and nothing it professes to condemn with such severity as the pursuit of wealth.

BELLE: You fear the world too much. All your other hopes have merged into the hope of being beyond its sordid reproach. I have seen your nobler aspirations fall off one by one, until the master-passion, Gain, engrosses you.

YOUNG SCROOGE: What then? So I have grown wiser in my years, what of it? I am not changed towards you. Am I?

BELLE: The contract that binds us is an old one, Ebenezer. It was made when we were both young and poor and content to be so, until, in good season, we could improve our worldly fortune by our patient industry. But you are changed. Your own feeling tells you that you are not what you were. Nor, perhaps, am I. That which promised happiness when we were one in heart, is fraught with misery now that we are two. How often I have thought of this or how long, I will not say. It is enough that I have thought of it, and can release you.

YOUNG SCROOGE: Have I ever sought release?

BELLE: In words. No. Never.

YOUNG SCROOGE: In what, then?

BELLE: In a changed nature; in an altered spirit; in another atmosphere of life; with another Hope as its great end. In everything that made my love of any worth or value in your sight. Tell me, Ebenezer, if this had never been between us, would you seek me out and try to win me now?

(Pause)

YOUNG SCROOGE: You think not?

BELLE: I would gladly think otherwise if I could. Heaven knows. But if you were free today, tomorrow, yesterday, can even I believe that you would choose a dowerless girl—you who weigh everything in increments of gain. Or, choosing her, do I not know that your repentance and regret would surely follow? I do; and I release you. With a full heart, for the love of him you once were. May you be happy in the life you have chosen. *(She exits.)*

YOUNG SCROOGE: The choice was never mine.

(The vision fades.)

MARLEY: You can't blame me for that! You heard the girl. It was his choice.

DIMINUTIVE GHOST: But you left him little of one to make.

MARLEY: It's her fault. If she had stuck by him, as she should have, he could have had wealth *and* happiness.

DIMINUTIVE GHOST: So wealth alone does not constitute happiness?

MARLEY: If he had invested his money in those pursuits which bring happiness, he could have had as much of it as any man.

DIMINUTIVE GHOST: Is that what you did? Invested in happy pursuits? Or did you reinvest every dividend in further investments. An endless cycle of profit for profit's sake with no conceivable end in sight.

MARLEY: Are we here to dispute my business practices? Because I'll gladly weigh my portfolio against any man's living, if that's the game.

DIMINUTIVE GHOST: Yes, you were always an able businessman, Jacob Marley.

MARLEY: I am glad to hear you admit it.

DIMINUTIVE GHOST: I have one question, though. You didn't need him. Why didn't you let him go?

MARLEY: You saw that I did. The decision was his to stay.

DIMINUTIVE GHOST: But you could have forced him out. You could have made him leave. You would have been twice as wealthy. Twice as powerful. Twice as feared and hated. But instead you bound him further to you at every step, and drove her away.

(Pause)

MARLEY: ...I didn't want to be alone.

(MARLEY *seems on the verge of tears. The* PHANTOM *offers him a handkerchief.*)

DIMINUTIVE GHOST: What is it that misery loves, your honor?

(*The* GIANT GHOST *nods.*)

GIANT GHOST: Well, if there is nothing further from the prosecution?

DIMINUTIVE GHOST: Just one more thing.

MARLEY: No, Spirit, please, show me no more. Why do you delight to torture me? I will stipulate that I have been a degenerate soul in every aspect, only let these remembrances be over.

DIMINUTIVE GHOST: Just one shadow more, your honor. It goes to motive.

MARLEY: No more, I don't wish to see it. Show me no more.

GIANT GHOST: I will allow it.

DIMINUTIVE GHOST: Exhibit C!

(MARLEY's office. YOUNG MARLEY is hard at work at his desk when his sister MARGARET rushes in, nine months pregnant, and excitedly waving a letter in the air.)

MARGARET: Jacob! Jacob!

MARLEY: It's my sister, Margaret!

YOUNG MARLEY: Maggie! What are you doing out of bed? You're in no condition.

MARGARET: It's a letter! It's from Toby, I know it! (Showing him the letter) That's the curve of his hand, isn't it? And that big one's a "C" as in Cratchit, I know it is. It must be from him!

YOUNG MARLEY: Yes, and who else would be sending you a letter from America?

MARGARET: Read it, will you, Jake? Read it to me! He's sent for me, I know it. He's sent for me to come join him.

YOUNG MARLEY: You know so much about his letters, I don't know why you bother me with reading them.

MARGARET: Oh, please, Jake! I'll sit quietly this time.

YOUNG MARLEY: Very well. *(He opens the letter.)* It says...

BOTH: "My Dearest Margaret..."

YOUNG MARLEY: Maggie!

MARGARET: I'll be quiet.

YOUNG MARLEY: "My heart aches with cruel longing each moment we're apart. Your precious lips—" You don't have a lady friend who can read these to you?

MARGARET: Jake!

YOUNG MARLEY: It's indecent.

MARGARET: Oh, go on. What does it say?

YOUNG MARLEY: Well, there are several embarrassing passages about the roundness of your...eyes.

MARGARET: He does go on about my eyes since he's been away.

YOUNG MARLEY: He asks about the baby.

MARGARET: *(Shouting into the letter)* He's fine! We're going to name him Bob!

YOUNG MARLEY: Ugh. What a stupid name.

MARGARET: Read! Read!

YOUNG MARLEY: He asks about me.

MARGARET: See? He does like you.

YOUNG MARLEY: And then he rambles on about— *(He falls silent as he reads ahead.)*

MARGARET: What? What is he rambling about?

(YOUNG MARLEY *abruptly puts the letter down.*)

YOUNG MARLEY: Nothing. *(He folds it back into its envelope.)*

MARGARET: What is it? Jacob, you tell me or, so help me, I'll find someone else to do it. There must be someone around this counting-house who knows how to read. (*Shouting upstairs*) Ebenezer!

YOUNG MARLEY: He's sent for you. He wants you to join him.

MARGARET: What?

YOUNG MARLEY: He's got himself a job in a foundry. He wants you to come to America to live.

MARGARET: Oh, I knew it! Didn't I know it? Jake, this is wonderful news!

YOUNG MARLEY: No, it's not wonderful! You're nine months pregnant. You're not going out on a ship, in the middle of winter, to sail across the ocean, to *live forever*, because this hooligan has finally *sent* for you. I forbid it. Have you no self-respect, Maggie?

MARGARET: No, I don't! And I don't want any if it keeps me away from my Toby one day longer. And if you had any self-respect for me, you would let me go with your blessing. I will be with him whether you like it or not, Jacob Marley!

YOUNG MARLEY: Well, I don't like it, and I won't pay for it. If he really wants to be with you, then he shall have to come back here to fetch you, or send the money himself to ship you there, for I'll not do it. And I'm writing him to tell him so.

(YOUNG MARLEY *immediately sits down and starts writing a letter.* MARGARET *is frantic.*)

MARGARET: Don't you dare!

YOUNG MARLEY: Think of the baby, Maggie. The passage to America is a treacherous crossing. Especially in winter. You could both die. Had you thought of that? At least, wait until the child is born. And had a few years to grow. *Then* we can talk about sending one of you over there.

MARGARET: I will wait until my baby is born, and then we're both getting on the first boat to anywhere but here. And we're naming him Bob! *(She storms out.)*

DIMINUTIVE GHOST: Your sister never did make it to America.

MARLEY: No. She died just after the child was born. So you see I was right. She never would have survived an ocean voyage in her state.

DIMINUTIVE GHOST: Except that she died of a broken heart. When you explained to her that passage for two would be twice as expensive as one.

MARLEY: Yes, and then I was stuck with the expense of raising the boy when his worthless father failed to retrieve him.

DIMINUTIVE GHOST: Well, he wouldn't have, would he?

(Reading from the letter YOUNG MARLEY *is writing)*

DIMINUTIVE GHOST: Not after you told him they had both died in a rail accident.

MARLEY: Tobias Cratchit was a reckless boy who was never going to amount to anything!

DIMINUTIVE GHOST: And yet he didn't amount to precisely nothing either, did he? He saved his earnings and purchased a small acreage in Virginia and farmed it for many years with his children from a second marriage. Bob might have been happy there.

MARLEY: Bob is doing just fine here in London. Where he belongs. He has honest employment. A tolerable pretty wife, so I am told. One or two children, I think.

DIMINUTIVE GHOST: Yes, you've kept a keen eye out for him, haven't you?

MARLEY: I will not stomach the blame for Toby Cratchit being a negligent father. I give you that I am no saint, but I provided for my nephew as best I could.

DIMINUTIVE GHOST: A minimum wage job in your counting-house? Is that the best you could do? A dilapidated house on a patch of reclaimed swamp you were unable to sell at market? You didn't even have the foresight to leave him anything in your will.

MARLEY: I didn't leave a will, and you know it. It puts ideas into people's heads. Nothing makes a family so eager to see you dead, as knowing how they will profit by your demise.

DIMINUTIVE GHOST: And as a result, all of your belongings reverted to your partner at your passing. So Bob will never see a penny of it.

MARLEY: And now who's weighing money as a measure of happiness?

DIMINUTIVE GHOST: I wouldn't say that. But it can be a measure of generosity.

MARLEY: Who are you to say what makes my nephew happy? I am all the family he has now. And I won't have a quorum of ghosts and phantasms telling me what's best for him by committee when I can see it plainly for myself, thank you.

GIANT GHOST: Of course you can. So have a look.

(The GIANT GHOST *waves its arm and they are transported to...)*

*(*BOB CRATCHIT's *living room.)*

MARLEY: Where is this?

GIANT GHOST: Bob Cratchit's house, of course. Perhaps you would recognize it better... If you'd ever set foot in it!

MARLEY: I don't pry into my employees' personal lives.

GIANT GHOST: You mean, your *nephew's?*

MARLEY: Yes. That's what I said.

(A woman comes in from the outdoors, bundled against the cold in a heavy shawl.)

JENNY: Hello?

GIANT GHOST: And who's this?

MARLEY: Aha! That's his wife. You thought I wouldn't recognize her.

(The woman removes her shawl. It is BOB's *former assistant,* JENNY.*)*

JENNY: Mrs Cratchit? Bob?

MARLEY: Why it's that ill-mannered girl, Jenny!

(Several CRATCHIT CHILDREN *burst in from the next room.)*

CHILDREN: Jenny! It's Jenny!

MARLEY: What's she doing in Bob Cratchit's house?

*(*MRS CRATCHIT *comes in from the kitchen.)*

MRS CRATCHIT: Is that Jenny?

CHILDREN: Here's Jenny, mother! Hurrah! There's such a goose, Jenny.

MRS CRATCHIT: Why, bless your heart alive, my dear, how late you are. You weren't as late last Christmas Day by half-an-hour. We were starting to think you weren't coming.

JENNY: The milliner give us a good deal of work extra to finish up last night, and had to clear away this morning.

MRS CRATCHIT: I don't know why you let them work you to death so.

JENNY: I'm lucky to be apprenticed anywhere at all after Mister Scrooge blackened my good name all over town.

MRS CRATCHIT: Aye, that old scoundrel's a bad mark on any reference. Well, never mind, so long as you are come. Sit ye down before the fire, my dear, and have a warm, Lord bless ye.

JENNY: Where's Mister Cratchit?

MRS CRATCHIT: He's out with our Tiny Tim. They'd have been back by now, but Bob was late home from work again and you know how that story goes. Tim still wanted to go for his walk along the commons, though. And it's for his health, so off they went.

(They hear BOB coming up the walk, singing a Christmas carol.)

CHILDREN: There's father coming!

MRS CRATCHIT: And here they come. Quick, Jenny, hide, hide.

(JENNY hides, and MRS CRATCHIT assumes a somber expression, as BOB comes in carrying TINY TIM on his shoulders.)

MARLEY: Is that Tiny Tim? Why is he limping?

GIANT GHOST: The boy is lame since birth. That's how he walks.

MARLEY: Well, he should stop it. It's disconcerting.

(BOB sets TINY TIM down, rubbing his hands together for warmth.)

BOB: Where's our Jenny? Any news yet?

MRS CRATCHIT: Not coming.

BOB: Not coming? Not coming upon Christmas Day? Oh, I knew it. They work her harder, every year. It was only a matter of time before she could not come at all. That's the cold reality and there's nothing for it.

(JENNY *comes out of hiding prematurely and gives* BOB *a hug.*)

JENNY: Oh, now, Bob Cratchit. You know I wouldn't let a wee thing like reality intrude upon your holiday cheer. I haven't missed a Christmas since the year you took me in after Mister Scrooge put me out in the street. And I shan't miss another one yet as long as you'll have me.

MRS CRATCHIT: You know there's always room for one more at our table, dear. Now, won't you help out in the kitchen a moment?

(JENNY *heads into the kitchen, trailing a procession of* CRATCHIT CHILDREN *behind her.*)

MRS CRATCHIT: And how did little Tim behave?

BOB: As good as gold, and better. Somehow he gets thoughtful, sitting by himself so much, and thinks the strangest things you ever heard. He told me, coming home, that he hoped the people in the church saw him, because he was a cripple, and it might be pleasant to them to remember upon Christmas Day, who made lame beggars walk, and blind men see. (*He tries to smile, but he looks as though he'd rather cry.*) You know, I think Tiny Tim has grown strong and hearty these past few weeks. It must be the holiday upon us. He lives for this day.

MRS CRATCHIT: Yes, dear. Come, get yourself ready for dinner.

(BOB *becomes cheerful again.*)

BOB: Ready? Ha! When has a dinner ever caught me unawares? (*He playfully strikes a pugilistic pose.*) But is the *dinner* ready for *me*?

(JENNY *bursts in, almost knocking him over, with the Christmas goose on a tray. It is quite possibly the smallest Christmas goose in history.*)

JENNY: Well, here's the goose!

BOB: Oh! And such a goose! Magnificent! There never was such a goose. I don't believe there ever was such a goose cooked.

(MRS CRATCHIT *and* JENNY *hurry in and out of the kitchen, bearing forth trays of food.*)

MRS CRATCHIT: And apple sauce!

JENNY: And mashed potatoes!

TINY TIM: And gravy!

(TINY TIM *proudly brings in a tureen of gravy last.*)

MRS CRATCHIT: And all of it steeped in onions and sage.

BOB: And the size of the goose!

MRS CRATCHIT: I got a bargain of a price for it.

BOB: It looks delicious.

MRS CRATCHIT: And tender! Wait till you taste it, Bob.

BOB: I don't need to, I am half-full just from the smell of it.

MRS CRATCHIT: Well, don't forget to save room for dessert, for there's a...

ALL: Great...! Scrumptious...!

(MRS CRATCHIT *dashes into the kitchen and returns with a small pudding.*)

ALL: Pudding!!

JENNY: Oh, a pudding!

TINY TIM: A wonderful pudding.

MRS CRATCHIT: Is it wonderful?

BOB: Why, Mrs Cratchit, I regard it as the single greatest achievement of our marriage.

MRS CRATCHIT: I was so worried it wouldn't turn out. There wasn't enough flour, to begin with. And the price of spices. I hope it's done enough.

BOB: It's perfect!

MRS CRATCHIT: Is it?

BOB: Gather round, everyone. Children, gather round. Feast your eyes—

MRS CRATCHIT: Just your eyes, now, Tim.

BOB: —on this Great Scrumptious Pudding and tell me, if there is anyone among you who can say why this pudding should not be eaten... Let 'em speak now...

(They all join in...)

ALL: And Father shall have your piece!

(They all laugh at his annual joke, as they sit down to dinner.)

TINY TIM: A toast! Papa, give a toast.

MRS CRATCHIT: *(Laughing and groaning)* Ohh, no toasts.

BOB: Let's see. What shall it be? Aha! To Mister Scrooge!

MRS CRATCHIT: Scrooge?

BOB: *(Raising his glass)* I give you Mister Scrooge, the Founder of the Feast.

MRS CRATCHIT: The Founder of the Feast indeed! I wish I had him here. I'd give him a piece of my mind to feast upon, and I hope he'd have a good appetite for it.

BOB: My dear, the children. Christmas Day.

MRS CRATCHIT: It should be Christmas Day, I am sure, on which one drinks the health of such an odious, stingy, hard, unfeeling man as Mister Scrooge. You

know he is, Robert. Nobody knows it better than you
do, poor fellow.

BOB: My dear, Christmas Day.

MRS CRATCHIT: I'll give you a day to name me one
good thing that has ever come of that man.

(*Uncomfortable silence*)

JENNY: Well... It would be thanks to Mister Scrooge
that I came to share my Christmases with you...
in a roundabout way.

(BOB *smiles awkwardly.*)

MRS CRATCHIT: Very well, I'll drink his health for
your sake and the Day's, not for his. Long life to him.
A merry Christmas and a happy new year. He'll be
very merry and very happy, I have no doubt.

TINY TIM: Please, Momma, we mustn't quarrel.

JENNY: Mister Cratchit will give us a different toast.
Won't you, Bob?

(BOB *raises his glass again, somewhat disheartenedly.*)

BOB: To absent friends then.

TINY TIM: To Grandma and Grampa!

BOB: There you are. To Grandmother Cratchit.
May she rest in peace.

TINY TIM: And Grandpa.

BOB: Yes... to my father. Wherever he is.

TINY TIM: And great uncle Marley.

MRS CRATCHIT: Enough, Tim.

(*Pause.* BOB *raises his glass with determination.*)

BOB: To my Uncle Jake. He was a kind...a kind of
man...who words cannot describe.

(MRS CRATCHIT *slams down her glass.*)

MRS CRATCHIT: Oh, I ask you.

BOB: He got us this house.

MRS CRATCHIT: He got us this great mortgage of a house.

BOB: Still, it's a roof over us.

MRS CRATCHIT: Aye, and pocked full of holes. *(Toasting)* And here's to the wind for blowing in at the cracks in our walls. And the ice for freezing shut the front door again. And here's to Sickness and Poverty and Hardship for taking the time out of their busy holiday to dine especially with us on a Christmas Day. *(She rounds on* BOB.*)* Must we do this every year? A kind word for everyone who's ever wronged you? The father who abandoned you. The uncle who raised you in poverty while he trafficked in luxury. The employer who even now conspires to ruin our every holiday since.

BOB: No, didn't I tell you? He gave me the day off.

MRS CRATCHIT: Aye, for now. And you know he'll come calling first thing in the afternoon with a change of heart. And off you'll go.

BOB: Perhaps this year will be different.

MRS CRATCHIT: Don't you know who your enemies are, Bob? And who has harmed you?

BOB: I know that on this day, none of that matters. No harm—nothing but joy—can come to any of us, while we are all here, together, a family, in this house. For that's what Christmas truly is. A time to be charitable to those who give us none. Forgiving of those who deserve none. And rejoice in those blessings we have. In truth, I pity men like Mister Scrooge and Uncle Jake and my father. For they shall never know the simple good it does ones heart to be here in this house on Christmas Day with all of you. *(Raising his glass again)* A Merry Christmas to us all, my dears. God bless us.

ALL: God bless us!

BOB: Every one.

(As BOB *and the* CRATCHITS *drink their toast...)*

*(...*MARLEY *hangs his head in shame.)*

GIANT GHOST: He seems happy enough.

MARLEY: Happy! He's miserable! They're all hopelessly miserable and pathetic, and they don't even seem to know it! I suppose he thinks to put on a brave face in front of the children, but this is preposterous. Did you see the size of that goose? I've seen fatter drumsticks on a field mouse. And the pudding! Not enough for a morsel, let alone feed a whole family. This is no way to celebrate Christmas. Even I know that. Where are their ribbons and bows and wreaths of holly? To think that flesh of mine should be mired in such abject austerity. It sickens me to my core.

DIMINUTIVE GHOST: That could be the arsenic.

MARLEY: All right, you have won, Spirits. I concede my nephew would have fared better in life without the curse of having me for an uncle. What a plague I was. And now I suppose it falls to me to undo the harm I've done in Bob's life? Very well, I'll do it. It's what I deserve. Send me back and I'll set him straight at once. It won't take long. All he needs is some sound fiscal advice and planning.

GIANT GHOST: You are not going back.

MARLEY: What?

DIMINUTIVE GHOST: No.

(The PHANTOM *shakes its head, too.)*

MARLEY: What do you mean? That's the point of this, isn't it? You've shown me what a waste of life I've been. But there's still a chance to save this family from a similar fate.

GIANT GHOST: Even if we wanted to—

DIMINUTIVE GHOST: Which we don't.

GIANT GHOST: —It's been seven years since you were laid in the ground, Jacob Marley. If you were to emerge from the grave now, it could cause a general panic.

MARLEY: Seven years? When did this happen?

GIANT GHOST: I told you, time is relative here. We are backed up with case after case. And every one of them, just like you, hell-bent on overturning their rightful sentence.

MARLEY: But you must send me back. How can I repair the damage I've done if I'm not allowed a second chance?

GIANT GHOST: You've had a lifetime of second chances, Jacob Marley. Every moment you live. Every breath you take, a new road lies in front of you. And you wasted all of yours headed always down the single path which has led you here.

MARLEY: Then what good has it been to have a trial at all? If there's no chance for acquittal. Or leniency.

GIANT GHOST: The point of the trial was not to determine your guilt or innocence. That has always been a forgone conclusion. Our only purpose here is to ensure that you appreciate the gravity of your crimes. It does no good to punish a soul incapable of guilt or remorse. You would simply spend the afterlife feeling terribly self-righteous and put upon, and telling everyone you met how undeserved was your fate. But now that you understand, your sentence can begin.

(MARLEY's chains rise up again and descend around him.)

MARLEY: No, please, Spirits, have mercy. This cannot be how it ends. I've changed, can't you see that? I'll show you how I've changed. I'll do anything. Let me save one soul. Let me save Bob's. The things I could tell him about finance alone will set him on a road to success in no time.

DIMINUTIVE GHOST: The very nature of your offer shows how little you *have* changed.

MARLEY: I apologize, force of habit. But you must let me help. If this family's fate is even partly my doing, you must let me undo it.

GIANT GHOST: Your punishment is irrevocable, Jacob Marley. You are a selfish, covetous, misanthrope.

MARLEY: I was. I am. I know it. But what about Bob Cratchit and the children? And Reverend Hedges? And young Jenny? What about Tiny Tim? You can't let him suffer for my selfishness.

DIMINUTIVE GHOST: You needn't worry. He won't suffer long.

MARLEY: What? What do you mean by that? Spirit?

GIANT GHOST: *(To the others)* Our time is almost done.

MARLEY: Answer me, Spirit. Tell me if Tiny Tim will live.

(The PHANTOM gestures at MARLEY and lightning flashes in the sky. MARLEY becomes entranced with a vision.)

MARLEY: I see a vacant seat in the poor chimney-corner, and a crutch without an owner, carefully preserved.

GIANT GHOST: If these shadows remain unaltered by the Future, the child will die.

MARLEY: No, no! Oh, no, unkind Spirit, say he will be spared.

DIMINUTIVE GHOST: If these shadows remain unaltered by the Future, no other Christmases will find him here.

MARLEY: No, he can't die! You must let me intervene. Not for my sake, Spirit, for *theirs*.

GIANT GHOST: I know you believe your intentions are sincere. But you have corrupted everything you have ever touched. Yours is a toxic spirit, Jacob Marley. But you will not poison another soul. *(To the others)* Let us go.

MARLEY: And Tim, poor tiny Tim? He's just a boy. A very small and sickly boy. Will you walk away from him, too? Is that Justice?

GIANT GHOST: No, it is not. But it is your interference that has brought them to this pass. For better or worse, you shall have no more discourse with this family. They are finally free of you. Their fates, however dismal or brief, are finally in their own hands. Not yours.

(They turn their backs on him with grim finality, and start to walk away.)

MARLEY: ...Then let me save Scrooge.

(The three departing spirits stop in their tracks.)

GIANT GHOST: Scrooge?

DIMINUTIVE GHOST: Ebenezer Scrooge?

(The PHANTOM *gestures quizzically.)*

MARLEY: You said yourself he is already irreparably doomed to a fate worse than mine. He cannot be corrupted. What further harm could I do?

GIANT GHOST: But why would you want to help the man who murdered you?

MARLEY: Because every life on this earthly sphere impacts on every other. If even one soul can be enlightened by this night, then for all we know the whole of London may shine brighter tomorrow.

DIMINUTIVE GHOST: But *Scrooge*? He is beyond hope.

MARLEY: No. It is never too late to change. I know that now more than any creature living or deceased. For look at me, I was seven years dead before I saw the error of my ways. But I have, Spirits, I've seen it. And now I know that no soul is past repair. Even mine. Even his. I know it, even if you have forgot. Give me a chance, Spirits. Give him a chance. And give yourselves a chance. For if beings such as yourselves cannot see the faintest glimmer of Possibility in a person, then all hope is truly lost. But we are not yet at that point of despair, because *I* at least have hope. I, of all people. And if I can do nothing else, I can do this.

DIMINUTIVE GHOST: But he killed you.

MARLEY: Bah! What care I for that? Death is the best thing that ever happened to me. Let me speak to him. I know he will listen. I will tell him what has happened to me, and the visions I have seen.

GIANT GHOST: No. There are higher powers than we, Jacob Marley. And it is forbidden for the likes of you to reveal to the living anything that has transpired here.

(The PHANTOM *tugs at the* DIMINUTIVE GHOST'*s elbow. The* DIMINUTIVE GHOST *nods, and nudges the* GIANT GHOST.*)*

DIMINUTIVE GHOST: ...But we could show him.

MARLEY: Yes, that's the spirit, Spirits! Show him but a piece of what I have seen tonight, these shadows of our past and present, and the future, and he may yet find it in his heart to change as I have done. I beg you. While there's still a chance.

(Pause. The spirits exchange dubious glances.)

GIANT GHOST: He will not believe us. He will think it is a hoax. They always do.

MARLEY: He will believe me. Trust me, Spirits, I know this man as I know my very self, and he will receive your visits in the spirit they are given, or you may damn me twice.

GIANT GHOST: Very well, but there is precious little time. Sepak to your friend, Jacob Marley. If he can open his heart enough to receive our visits... There may be hope for us all.

MARLEY: I will.

(The PHANTOM *approaches* MARLEY *and raises its arms in a silent wail, shaking its fists in a terrifying manner, as if rattling chains.* MARLEY *is unnerved by this, but tries to be polite.)*

MARLEY: Yes, thank you for that.

(Without another word, the three spirits disappear into shadows and MARLEY *finds himself standing on...)*

3. THE HAUNTING OF SCROOGE

(A busy street in London)

MARLEY: Thank you, Spirits! You will not regret this! I will see to it that you don't!

*(*PASSERSBY *come and go on the street, cheerfully greeting each other as they pass.)*

PASSERBY: Merry Christmas to you!

SECOND PASSERBY: And you, as well!

MARLEY: It's still Christmas! There's still time.

*(*MARLEY *skips and dances among them, unseen, but happy to be there.)*

THIRD PASSERBY: Merry Christmas!

FOURTH PASSERBY: Merry Christmas!

MARLEY: Merry Christmas!! Hee hee! Merry Christmas, indeed. The merriest Christmas of all! But first I've got to find Scrooge. Now where would he be at this hour?

(*As if in answer to the question,* SCROOGE *trudges by, just then, eyes downcast, trying to avoid the other* PASSERSBY.)

FIFTH PASSERBY: Merry Christmas to ye!

SCROOGE: Christmas is a humbug!

(MARLEY *rushes toward* SCROOGE, *tripping on his chains.*)

MARLEY: Scrooge! Scrooge, my old partner!

(SCROOGE *walks away without acknowledging him.*)

MARLEY: Scrooge? Scrooge! (*Shaking his chains in frustration*) SCROOOOGE!!

(*But* SCROOGE *is gone.*)

MARLEY: He doesn't hear me! I am invisible. And inaudible. And intangible. Is this some further torment? How can I haunt the man when he cannot even hear me?

(*Just then,* SCROOGE *comes back in, looking perplexed.*)

SCROOGE: Did someone say something to me?

(*The* PASSERSBY *shrug.*)

FIFTH PASSERBY: Merry Christmas?

SCROOGE: Humbug! (*He storms out again.*)

MARLEY: Scrooge, wait!

(MARLEY *gets up and runs after him, stumbling in his chains.*)

(SCROOGE's *front doorstep. There is a blind* BEGGAR *panhandling in front of the building.*)

BEGGAR: Alms? Alms for a poor, and a blind, and a cripple— Merry Christmas to ye.

(SCROOGE *trudges in, followed by* MARLEY, *who is desperately trying to get his attention.*)

MARLEY: Ebenezer, please. Ebenezer!

SCROOGE: *(To himself)* Here we are.

BEGGAR: Alms, sir?

SCROOGE: Get away from me, you vermin! *(Fumbles for his keys)* Where are my keys?

MARLEY: Oh, you mustn't go inside. I don't know if I can get through a door. These accursed chains. Ebenezer!

(SCROOGE *finds his key and starts up the steps.*)

MARLEY: No, Ebenezer. Listen to me. Ebenezer. *(In desperation, he lunges in front of* SCROOGE *and flings himself against the door, blocking the way with his arms outstretched.)* EBENEZER!!

(Suddenly, SCROOGE *looks as if he's seen a ghost.)*

SCROOGE: Marley!

MARLEY: *(Relieved)* Yes, it's me.

(But SCROOGE, *again, can't see* MARLEY. *He feels the door knocker, instead.)*

SCROOGE: Jacob?

BEGGAR: Sir? Is there something the matter, sir?

SCROOGE: I thought for a moment I was in the presence of my old partner Jacob Marley who's been dead these seven years.

MARLEY: But you are. I'm right here. We have to talk.

BEGGAR: You mean, you saw a ghost?

SCROOGE: What? No! Humbug! *(He fumbles for his key again.)*

BEGGAR: You're sure you don't need help getting up to your room, sir?

SCROOGE: So you can rob me? Bah! Get away from my doorstep before I summon a constable. *(He goes inside, slams the door shut, and loudly bolts several locks behind him.)*

MARLEY: *(To the* BEGGAR*)* He didn't mean that. *(To* SCROOGE*)* But you *can* hear me. ...Somehow. *(He lifts his arms and rattles his chains a bit, finally realizing that they are the source of his power.)* So I can be heard. I *will* be heard! *(He rattles his chains and lets out a ghostly bellow...)* EBENEZER!

(As MARLEY *raises his arms, the sky darkens and, with a gesture,* SCROOGE*'s door is flung open.* MARLEY *laughs aloud as he strides triumphantly into the house, no longer tripping over his own chains. The* BEGGAR *looks like he's seen a ghost now, or heard one, anyway.)*

BEGGAR: Bit drafty hereabouts, anyway. *(He quickly gathers up his things and scurries away.)*

*(*SCROOGE*'s bedroom.* SCROOGE *comes in, changing into his bedclothes, mumbling to himself.)*

SCROOGE: A bit of undigested beef, no doubt.

*(*MARLEY *comes in through the wall behind* SCROOGE. *He rattles his chains.)*

MARLEY: Ebenezer!

*(*SCROOGE *turns with a start, just as* MARLEY *puts the chains down, disappearing from* SCROOGE*'s sight.)*

SCROOGE: ...Humbug!

*(*MARLEY *approaches him from the other side and rattles his chains again.)*

MARLEY: Scrooge!!

(SCROOGE *turns, but again,* MARLEY *gives him only a glimpse before disappearing.*)

SCROOGE: It's humbug still! I won't believe it.

(SCROOGE *climbs into his bed, huddles fearfully under the covers. Rising out of the headboard,* MARLEY *springs into bed with him, shaking his chains more frighteningly than ever.*)

MARLEY: Ebenezer Scrooge!

SCROOGE: How now! What do you want with me?

MARLEY: Ha ha ha! Much!

SCROOGE: Who are you?

MARLEY: Do you not recognize me? Then ask me who I was.

SCROOGE: Who were you then? You're particular, for a shade.

MARLEY: In life I was your partner, Jacob Marley.

SCROOGE: Humbug, I tell you! Humbug! I saw you buried.

MARLEY: You *had* me buried!

SCROOGE: I don't know what you mean by that. I don't know why you're here. In fact, you are not here at all. You're nothing but thin air.

MARLEY: Why do you doubt your senses?

SCROOGE: They are easily deceived. Very little things affect them. Slight disorders of the stomach. Fits of fever.

MARLEY: Pangs of guilty conscience?

SCROOGE: Conscience? Why should conscience be—?

MARLEY: You know what you have done!

(MARLEY *shakes his chains and gives a frightful cry.*)

SCROOGE: Mercy! Dreadful apparition, why do you trouble me?

MARLEY: Man of the worldly mind! Do you believe in me or not?

SCROOGE: I do. I must. But why do spirits walk the earth, and why do they come to me?

MARLEY: Because it is required of every man that the spirit within him should walk abroad among his fellowmen, and travel far and wide; and if that spirit goes not forth in life, it is condemned to do so after death. It is doomed to wander through the world— oh, woe is me!—and witness what it cannot share, but might have shared on earth, and turned to happiness!

(MARLEY *raises another cry and shakes his chains. To* SCROOGE, *he is terrifying, but it is clear that* MARLEY *is also having almost too much fun.*)

SCROOGE: You are fettered. Tell me why?

MARLEY: I wear the chain I forged in life. I made it link by link, and yard by yard. I girded it on of my own free will, and of my own free will I wore it. Is its pattern familiar to you? Or would you know the weight and length of the strong coil you bear yourself? It was full as heavy and as long as this, seven Christmas Eves ago. You have laboured on it, since. It is a ponderous chain!

SCROOGE: Jacob, Old Jacob Marley, tell me more. Speak comfort to me, Jacob!

MARLEY: I have none to give. Nor can I tell you what I would. A very little more, is all permitted to me. I cannot rest, I cannot linger in this place. My spirit never walked beyond our counting-house—mark me!— in life my spirit never roved beyond the narrow limits of our money-changing hole. Oh! captive, bound, and

double-ironed, not to know, the futility of incessant
labour. Not to know that any Christian spirit working
kindly in its little sphere, whatever it may be, will find
its mortal life too short for its vast means of usefulness.
Not to know that no space of regret can make amends
for one life's opportunity misused! Yet such was I! Oh!
Such was I!

SCROOGE: But you were always a good man of business,
Jacob.

MARLEY: Business! Mankind was my business! The
common welfare was my business. Charity, mercy,
forbearance, and benevolence, were, all, my business.
The dealings of my trade were but a drop of water in
the comprehensive ocean of my business! Why did I
walk through crowds of fellow-beings with my eyes
turned down, and never raise them to that blessed Star
which led the Wise Men to a poor abode! Were there no
poor homes to which its light would have conducted
me! But hear me! My time is nearly gone.

SCROOGE: I will. I will, Jacob! Pray!

MARLEY: I am here tonight to warn you, that you have
yet a chance and hope of escaping my fate. A chance
and hope of my procuring, Ebenezer.

SCROOGE: You were always a good friend to me.
Thank 'ee!

MARLEY: I was nothing to you!

SCROOGE: Yes, Jacob.

MARLEY: You will be haunted by Three Spirits.

SCROOGE: Is that the chance and hope you mentioned,
Jacob?

MARLEY: It is.

SCROOGE: I—I think I'd rather not.

MARLEY: Without their visits, you cannot hope to shun the path I tread. This is an opportunity for you.

SCROOGE: *(Nervously) Yes, I see that... Well, then...*

*(*SCROOGE *swallows hard. He nods, fearfully.* MARLEY *grins.)*

MARLEY: Expect the first tonight, when the bell tolls One. Expect the second tomorrow at the same hour. And the third upon the following night.

SCROOGE: Couldn't I take 'em all at once, and have it over, Jacob?

*(*MARLEY *laughs.)*

MARLEY: Be careful what you wish for, Ebenezer. It is the season for giving, and there is no reason why a damnéd soul should not have that which will only increase his suffering.

SCROOGE: Eh? What do you mean by that?

MARLEY: Do you consent to these visitations?

SCROOGE: Yes, yes, I must!

MARLEY: Then look to see me no more; and look that, for your own sake, you remember what has passed between us!

SCROOGE: I will!

MARLEY: Heed my warning! Do not follow my course!

SCROOGE: I will! I won't!

*(*MARLEY *thrusts out his hand and* SCROOGE'*s bedroom disappears into the wall, and the wall disappears into vapour.)*

(The three spirits come in.)

GIANT GHOST: You have done well, Jacob Marley.

MARLEY: What will happen after this?

DIMINUTIVE GHOST: That remains to be seen.

GIANT GHOST: The rest is up to us.

DIMINUTIVE GHOST: And Ebenezer Scrooge, of course.

GIANT GHOST: But you have played your vital role.

DIMINUTIVE GHOST: If there were rewards for such acts as this, you would have earned yours tonight, Jacob Marley. But there are none.

MARLEY: Spirits, what is to become of me now?

GIANT GHOST: You already know the answer to that. You must walk the earth, Jacob Marley.

DIMINUTIVE GHOST: In the chains you have wrought, walk the earth.

GIANT GHOST: *(Shaking his hand)* Goodbye, Jacob Marley. Look to see us no more.

DIMINUTIVE GHOST: *(Shaking his hand)* May you rest in peace. Though we know you will not.

(The PHANTOM *starts to shake* MARLEY's *hand, then gives him a big hug instead. Then it points commandingly, sending him away.)*

MARLEY: Yes. Thank you. I... Well... Merry Christmas. *(He picks up his chains and shuffles out.)*

DIMINUTIVE GHOST: Bless me, but I pity him.

GIANT GHOST: How do you mean?

DIMINUTIVE GHOST: I think perhaps he could have been a good man after all. But what is he now?

GIANT GHOST: Doomed. To an eternity of wandering from door-to-door and place-to-place. Frequenting those haunts, where he himself will be haunted by guilt of his own misdeeds.

DIMINUTIVE GHOST: Seeking that which he could have had, but now will never find. A moment's comfort.

Peace of mind. A single place in this world, where he is not reviled and hated, or despised and forgotten.

GIANT GHOST: And rightly so. If he had wanted a refuge from the torments of this world, he should have built one for himself while he was in it. Jacob Marley has made his own deathbed. Now he must lie in it. Come, we have work to do.

(The three spirits begin to file out. The PHANTOM *lingers a moment longer, as if it still has one more vision to share...)*

4. BEDTIME FOR TINY TIM—(EPILOGUE)

*(*BOB CRATCHIT'*s house.* MRS CRATCHIT *is putting* TINY TIM *to bed.* MARLEY'*s ghost appears in the shadows of the room, unseen by either of them.)*

MRS CRATCHIT: Time for bed, Tim.

TINY TIM: Where's Poppa? Isn't he going to tuck me in?

MRS CRATCHIT: Your father has to work late tonight, Tim.

TINY TIM: But it's Christmas Eve. Will he be home tomorrow for Christmas?

MRS CRATCHIT: I don't know, he has a lot to do.

TINY TIM: But Mister Scrooge wouldn't make him work Christmas Day, would he, Momma?

(Pause)

MRS CRATCHIT: No, I'm sure he won't. Only a cruel, heartless, terrible man would make someone work on Christmas.

TINY TIM: You promise?

MRS CRATCHIT: Tim...just say your prayers.

*(*TINY TIM *kneels by his bed to pray.)*

TINY TIM: Now I lay me down to sleep. I pray the Lord my soul to keep. If I should die before I wake.... *(He stops praying.)* Momma? If I should die... Would I watch over you and Poppa?

MRS CRATCHIT: Tim! What kind of talk is that?

TINY TIM: Reverend Hedges says the people who've passed on are never really gone because they are always with us in spirit. And they keep watch over those of us living even after they're gone. Even if we don't know it.

MRS CRATCHIT: I suppose so. Do we have to talk about this now?

TINY TIM: I would watch over everyone.

MRS CRATCHIT: Tim, please! That's not going to happen.

TINY TIM: Do you think Grandma and Grandpa are watching over us?

MRS CRATCHIT: Well, your Grandpa Cratchit may still be alive.

TINY TIM: But when he's gone, he'll watch over us?

MRS CRATCHIT: *(Growing impatient)* Yes, Tim.

TINY TIM: What about Uncle Jacob?

MRS CRATCHIT: Oh, I don't know about Jacob Marley.

(TINY TIM *falls silent and looks disappointed, and after awhile, she can no longer bear it.)*

MRS CRATCHIT: All right, since it's Christmas... Yes, I'm sure he is.

TINY TIM: I think so, too.

(MARLEY, *in his corner, seems to brighten a little.)*

MRS CRATCHIT: Now finish your prayers.

TINY TIM: God bless Momma and Poppa and Jenny and Grandma. And Grandpa Cratchit.

MRS CRATCHIT: Wherever he is.

TINY TIM: And God bless Mister Scrooge and Reverend Hedges.

MRS CRATCHIT: And God bless everyone Tiny Tim can think of because he's trying to get out of going to bed.

TINY TIM: And Uncle Jacob?

(She is silent, and looks away. For a moment she seems to be looking directly at MARLEY, *but it's probably just a coincidence.)*

TINY TIM: ...Momma?

MRS CRATCHIT: Yes, yes, God bless Jacob Marley.

TINY TIM: God bless us every one.

*(*MRS CRATCHIT *puts her arm around* TINY TIM. *He puts his arm around her.* MARLEY *steps out of the shadows and puts his arms around them both.)*

THE END OF IT

.